fiona

(993
Annie)

Natural Causes

A black comedy

GW00771093

Eric Chappell

Samuel French — London
New York - Toronto - Hollywood

ISBN 978-0-573-01841-1

www.samuelfrench-london.co.uk

www.samuelfrench.com

FOR AMATEUR PRODUCTION ENQUIRIES

UNITED KINGDOM AND WORLD EXCLUDING NORTH AMERICA

plays@SamuelFrench-London.co.uk

020 7255 4302/01

Each title is subject to availability from Samuel French,

depending upon country of performance.

NATURAL CAUSES

First performed at the Theatre Royal, Windsor, on 20th
October, 1992 with the following cast:

Vincent	George Cole
Walter Bryce	Simon Williams
Angie	Karen Drury
Celia Bryce	Penny Morrell
Withers	Tyler Butterworth

Directed by Mark Piper
Designed by Alexander McPherson
Lighting by Mark Doubleday

CHARACTERS

Walter
Vincent
Angie
Celia
Withers

The action takes place in the study/library of Walter Bryce

ACT I
   SCENE 1   A morning in late spring
   SCENE 2   Midday

ACT II
   SCENE 1   Mid-afternoon
   SCENE 2   Evening — red sky at night

Time — the present

The extract from *Slough* by John Betjeman is reproduced by kind permission of John Murray (Publishers) Ltd.

Vincent – Barrie

Walter – This

Withers – Graham

Angie – Teresa

Celia – Sarah

ACT I
SCENE 1

Walter Bryce's study/library. A morning in late spring

It is a pleasant room overlooking a country garden, with an Adam fireplace and the walls lined with books. There is a desk by the french windows. A terrace with sunloungers is visible through the french windows. A large rubber plant stands in a corner of the room. There are a couple of easy chairs, a small sofa and a coffee table. There is an occasional table on which stands a drinks tray with assorted glasses

As the CURTAIN *rises, Walter Bryce enters from the hall. He is in his mid-forties and is dressed casually in a sweater and corduroy trousers. Vincent follows him in. He is a little older than Walter and is dressed more formally. At the moment he is wearing a rumpled raincoat and carrying what appears to be a medical bag. Despite the bag he somehow fails to achieve a proper professional manner and only succeeds in exuding an air of seedy menace, emphasized by Walter's obvious nervousness*

Vincent Sorry if I'm late, Mr Bryce — only I didn't realize you lived so far out.

Walter That's all right. Let me take your coat.

Vincent Thank you. Careful. Sandwiches in the pocket. *(He removes the sandwiches from his pocket)* I'll need to tuck into them — you don't mind?

Walter Er ... no.

Vincent *(sitting down with a sigh)* All morning on public transport — three changes — and then I couldn't get a cab at the station. You're looking at a piece of chewed string, Mr Bryce.

Walter Oh. Perhaps I should have met you ...

Vincent *(accusingly)* I wouldn't mind but I should be in Slough.

Walter Slough?

Vincent *(opening the sandwich bags)* I should have been in Slough two hours ago.

Walter (*lightly*) Well, never mind, you're here now. "Come friendly bombs and fall on Slough."

Vincent (*with a cold stare*) What?

Walter Er, it's a poem.

Vincent Oh. (*Pause*) Nothing against Slough, then?

Walter No.

Vincent A poem. Of course, I had you down for an intellectual as soon as I walked through that front door. I could smell the old books and leather bindings. I'm very susceptible to smell — which is unfortunate, really.

Walter (*politely*) Oh, why's that?

Vincent I live above a Chinese take-away, Mr Bryce — and it's no joke. Soya sauce, sweet and sour pork, fried rice. I knew a time when you had to go to China for that lot. (*Anxiously*) You can't smell it on me, can you?

Walter Er, no.

Vincent Good. I must say, it's nice to get away from it. (*He surveys the room*) You're living my dream, Mr Bryce.

Walter I beg your pardon?

Vincent I've always wanted a book-lined room in the country.

Walter Do you like books?

Vincent I've got a few — nothing like this. That was the first thing that struck me about this room — not a Penguin in sight.

Walter (*smiling*) I don't think it's cold enough, actually.

Vincent I was referring to the books. Of course I left school at fourteen. Educated at the end of the war. No chance.

Walter Er, no. Can I get you a drink, Mr ——?

Vincent Vincent. Thanks.

Walter Vincent. Is that your first or second name?

Vincent Both.

Walter (*surprised*) Vincent Vincent?

Vincent And neither.

Walter And neither?

Vincent We don't use our real names. Would you?

Walter No, I suppose not. Sherry?

Vincent Thank you. (*Pause*) I think Vincent's a good name.

Walter Yes. (*He pours two glasses of sherry*)

Vincent One of my colleagues calls himself Peaseblossom.

Walter Really?

Vincent Name of a fairy.

Walter I know.

Vincent *Twelfth Night.*

Walter *Midsummer Night's Dream.*

Vincent (*staring at him*) Are you sure?

Walter Yes.

Vincent Well, of course, I haven't had your advantages. I left school at fourteen, Mr Bryce. (*He studies him*) Minor public school?

Walter Yes.

Vincent And what do you do now?

Walter I write.

Vincent I could have been a writer. There's a book in me, Mr Bryce — if only they'd bothered to teach me English properly — it was the split infinitives and possessives that done for me. What do you write? Adventure stories? (*He begins to eat his sandwiches*)

Walter No. Historical biography.

Vincent History. Fascinating subject. Much maligned. Who said "When I hear the word history I reach for my revolver"?

Walter It was culture.

Vincent I thought it was Goering.

Walter He said it about culture.

Vincent Are you sure?

Walter Yes.

Vincent Were you a teacher?

Walter Yes.

Vincent Thought so. Hence the comprehensive knowledge — and the urge to correct people all the time.

Walter I'm sorry — I didn't mean to ——

Vincent No, that's all right. I hope you don't mind me chatting on like this but I do like to break the ice.

Walter No, I don't mind, but it wasn't quite what I expected.

Vincent Oh. Am I a disappointment?

Walter Disappointment?

Vincent Do you think I should have worn a darker tie? I would like to know.

Walter I hadn't really thought about it.

Vincent I have. After all, we are talking about ... death.

Walter Yes, I suppose we are.

Vincent Of course, you can take the image too far. I could hardly travel around with a scythe and an hourglass — not on public transport.

Walter (*smiling*) No.

Vincent There — I've made you smile, Mr Bryce.

Walter What?

Vincent That was my intention. I like to keep things light. I feel there should be a genuine lifting of the spirits at the approach of death — don't you agree?

Walter No. Actually, I find that rather difficult.

Vincent (*studying him*) Are you nervous?

Walter Yes.

Vincent Don't be. (*He drains his glass and begins to clean it with his handkerchief*)

Walter Er, I see you've removed your fingerprints, Vincent.

Vincent Well, I don't want to answer too many awkward questions, do I? The less anyone knows about my little visit the better — get my drift?

Walter Yes. Is it in the bag?

Vincent Yes. (*He smiles*) Do you want to see it?

Walter If you wouldn't mind.

Vincent opens the bag and proudly produces a small dark bottle

Oh. Is that it?

Vincent Is that it!? This is what separates me from the rest, Mr Bryce. Made from plants. With this I can assure you of a beautiful death. All perfectly natural. No chemicals. You go with dignity, you even look good — some say better.

Walter Is it strong?

Vincent Strong? It could stop an elephant!

Walter Quick?

Vincent Not unless you drink it neat — and I wouldn't recommend that. No, it's gradual — gives you time to walk around, have a chat, compose yourself. (*He takes a packet of crisps from the bag and opens it*) It also has the advantage of being colourless, odourless and virtually tasteless.

Walter But is it painless?

Vincent Well, I've never had any complaints. I can't personally vouch for the effect, but I wouldn't say it's painful. Your feet go cold, that's all.

Walter Feet?

Vincent It rises up through the body until it reaches the ... ticker.

Walter Oh. Anything else?

Vincent They don't say much after that.

Walter I see. Well, it all seems satisfactory. If you'd just leave the bottle ——

Vincent (*sharply*) Leave the bottle? I'm not a milkman, Mr Bryce. Leave the bottle — that's rich. I can't leave the bottle. Suppose it falls into the wrong hands?

Walter Oh — it was just that I thought you wanted to get to Slough.

Vincent Never mind about Slough. When would you like death to take place?

Walter (*casually*) Oh, as soon as possible.

Vincent Before lunch?

Walter That'll be fine.

Vincent (*hesitating*) Look, I didn't mean to rush you ——

Walter That's all right.

Vincent Don't you want to talk about it?

Walter Not really. Nothing to talk about.

Vincent (*curiously*) Do you believe in some sort of afterlife, Mr Bryce? (*He listens to the following with a crisp halfway to his mouth, faintly astonished*)

Walter Well, I suppose I do have some vague feeling of immortality — some timid hopes of a de-personalized afterlife. Something beyond the confines of space and matter — beyond the limits of comprehension — a sort of tidal, oceanic movement of humanity ——

Vincent Tidal? Oceanic? Well, I hope you can swim, Mr Bryce. Not thinking of coming back as a haddock, are you?

Walter You mean reincarnation.

Vincent (*sharply*) I know the word, Mr Bryce. Did I mention the fee? The fee is flexible — according to means — in fact we prefer to call it a donation.

Walter Of course. There's a cheque on the desk.

Vincent crosses to the desk and examines the cheque

Is that satisfactory?

Vincent Oh yes. More than satisfactory. Thank you. (*Pause*) You're sure you don't want to talk about it?

Walter Quite sure.

Vincent I think I would in your position. (*He looks out the window*) Nice view from the window. Rolling lawns, rock garden, gravel walks. Trout stream. Mr Bryce, what are those bushes down at the end?

Walter Which ones?

Vincent The yellow ones.

Walter (*looking out the window*) Forsythia.

While Walter looks out Vincent deftly pours some of the poison into his glass

Vincent I envy you, Mr Bryce.

Walter (*turning*) Do you have a garden?

Vincent Only a window box. I have this bedsitter in Shepherd's Bush. (*Looking around*) After all this, you don't think a de-personalized afterlife might prove something of a disappointment?

Walter Look, I don't wish to detain you any further, Vincent ...

Vincent Sorry. (*He sighs*) I just wish I hadn't mentioned Slough. Your drink, Mr Bryce. (*He hands Walter his glass of sherry*) And may I say that when I first arrived I thought you might have been wasting my time. I had you down for nervous and uncertain. I never realized you'd display such stoicism in the face of death.

Walter Yes, well, it isn't me who has to face it, is it?

Vincent (*staring at him*) What?

Walter I mean, it's my wife who has to take the stuff.

Vincent Your wife?

Walter Yes.

Vincent Are you sure?

Walter Yes.

Vincent Not you.

Walter No.

Vincent Don't move, Mr Bryce. I think there's something in your glass. (*He takes the drink from Walter and pours it into the base of the rubber plant*)

Walter watches him in horror

Walter My God! You were going to poison me.

Vincent A slight misunderstanding.

Walter A slight misunderstanding! I would have been dead.

Vincent I must have confused you with Slough. I'm sorry.

Walter You could have warned me. You're not very professional, are you?

Vincent On the contrary — I was being very professional. You don't think I was going to say, here's the poison — knock it back? No. When you go to the dentist you don't see the needle, do you? He holds it behind his back and talks about the weather and the family. How's the wife? How are the children? And then — bingo.

Walter Bingo! And on to Slough, leaving me on the carpet as dead as mutton.

Vincent Look, I said I was in error. If we can't admit our mistakes ... And after all, there's no real harm done — at worst I may have poisoned your rubber plant.

Walter Isn't that enough? Now if you'd just leave the bottle ——

Vincent I can't do that. I have to see her, Mr Bryce.

Walter Is that necessary?

Vincent Of course it's necessary. I'd like to point out that there are quite a few husbands in the Thames Valley with ambitions of becoming widowers. We have to be careful.

Walter Careful! You haven't been very careful up to now.

Vincent (*wincing*) I hope we're not going to keep harping on that, Mr Bryce. All I need to ascertain is that your wife is ready to go.

Walter Oh yes. She's been ready for years.

Vincent begins to clean the poison glass with a tissue

Vincent Why is that, Mr Bryce?

Walter Depression.

Vincent (*surprised*) Depression?

Walter Yes. What's the matter? Don't you touch depression?

Vincent Oh yes. We call it the Big D. (*Pause*) You mean she's depressed living here?

Walter Yes.

Vincent She should live in Shepherd's Bush. Just one question. If she's been ready for years — why has she never gone?

Walter Well, the trouble is — she's always wanted me to go with her.

Vincent What?

Walter It was my idea to get married — she'd have preferred a suicide pact.

Vincent I see. There'd have to be a note ——

Walter Plenty of notes. (*He produces a sheaf of papers*) Which would you prefer?

Vincent examines the letters

Vincent Oh no — these won't do at all — they're typed and unsigned.
(*Darkly*) You could have prepared these yourself.
Walter She likes to leave them in my typewriter. on my desk
Vincent And look at this: (*reading*) "Rain, rain, rain — I can't go on."
People don't kill themselves because it's raining, Mr Bryce.
Walter But I thought the final reason could often be quite trivial.
Vincent There's trivial and trivial. I just hope you're not wasting my time.
I had a client like this once before. Son of a butcher in West Finchley —
suddenly discovered he was homosexual. I was up and down on that
Northern Line for days while he made up his mind. The times he had that
glass to his lips ... the times he put it down again. Finally he decided to
live with it — come out of the closet and tell his parents everything. He's
alive today and living with a gent's hairdresser in Streatham. Mind you,
it wasn't a complete waste of time. When his father found out he took
it instead. Now, if you could fetch your wife ... (*He is about to throw the
tissue into the bin. Pause*) Oh. Do you have a dog?
Walter Yes.
Vincent Does he root about in the wastepaper baskets?
Walter Sometimes.
Vincent Then I suggest you burn this. (*He hands the tissue to Walter*)
Now I'd like to wash my hands — this stuff gets everywhere.
Walter (*distastefully*) Across the hall ...

Vincent exits to the hall

*Walter carries the tissue gingerly and throws it in the fireplace. He
examines his hands, hesitates, then wipes them on his handkerchief. He
hesitates, then throws the handkerchief into the fireplace*

*Angie enters the room. She is in her late twenties, attractive, with a
independent, strong-willed tilt to her chin*

She puts her hand on Walter's arm. He starts

Angie Has he gone?
Walter No — he's washing his hands.

Angie What's he like?

Walter He's not very intelligent. He thought he'd come for me. Apparently he's in a hurry to get to Slough.

Angie That could be a good thing.

Walter You ask the rubber plant if it's a good thing.

Angie It'll probably make him careless.

Walter It has done, Angie.

Angie I mean he won't ask too many questions.

Walter Don't you believe it. He's done nothing but ask questions since he arrived. He wants to meet her.

Angie Oh.

Walter Where is she?

Angie Still in bed.

Walter Oh no. Not today. I wanted her to have a last look around the garden.

Angie She's deep in depression, Walter.

Walter She's been deep in depression for over twenty years, Angie. And if this is going to be her last day I'd like her to see the tulips by the front wall — she's always been fond of tulips.

Angie Tulips! What's the point, Walter? She's fond of roses — perhaps she should hang on for those. And then there's the dahlias. It could be September before we get this done.

Walter I thought it might cheer her up.

Angie (*staring at him*) We're not trying to cheer her up, Walter. We don't want to give her a reason for staying, do we? Now, where's the stuff?

Walter I think he put it in his pocket. He won't leave it, Angie.

Angie I'll get it. What's his name?

Walter Vincent.

Angie First or second?

Walter Both.

Angie Vincent Vincent?

Walter And neither.

Angie Neither? It all sounds very strange.

Walter You think it's strange — we could have had Peaseblossom. I wish we'd never got mixed up with them.

Angie You're not getting cold feet, are you, Walter?

Walter No — it's Celia who's going to get the cold feet — and that's just the side effect.

Angie Walter — we've decided — we mustn't weaken now.

Walter No. *(Pause)* I wonder if she'd like to walk the dog.

Angie She doesn't want to get up. She's weary. She says she's tired of her body.

Walter *(irritably)* She's tired of her body — how does she think I feel?

Angie Well, I'm not tired of mine, Walter.

Walter *(ardently)* Neither am I.

They embrace

Angie After all, she wants to go.

Walter She wanted to go to Greece last year — hated every minute of it.

Angie But she's been preparing for this moment all her life — all we're doing is giving her a gentle push.

Walter It may be a gentle push but don't forget it's still an offence to counsel a person to suicide in this country. After all, we sent for this man. She won't like that. For years we've been saying don't do it — now we're shouting jump.

Angie Walter, we can't stop now. Ask yourself this — do you love me and do you want to be with me always?

Walter Yes.

Angie Then you've no choice.

They kiss

Walter *(starting)* God! He's in the garden.

Angie What's he doing?

Walter Probably looking for poisonous plants.

Angie Did he see us?

Walter I'm not sure.

Angie Go to Celia — make sure we're not disturbed.

Walter What are you going to do?

Angie Leave him to me.

Walter For God's sake be careful ...

He exits into the hall

Angie crosses and opens the french windows

Angie Hallo.

Vincent enters through the french windows

Vincent Just admiring the garden. I hope you don't mind?

Angie Not at all. I'm sorry if you've been kept waiting. I understand you're in a hurry to get to Slough.

Vincent It's not so much that I'm in a hurry to get to Slough — more that someone's in a hurry to leave it.

Angie Another client?

Vincent (*proudly*) University lecturer — in philosophy. Bit of a catch.

Angie He must be.

Vincent Yes. When he found that his wife had been unfaithful he didn't sit down and question the nature of reality. No — he hid all her clothes and locked her in the cellar. Now she's escaped and he's got nothing to live for. Philosophy has been given the elbow and he's turned to us.

Angie Then you must go at once. Let me have the bare bodkin and you can be on your way.

Vincent (*staring at her*) Bare what?

Angie Bodkin. (*Pause*) It's a dagger.

Vincent (*sharply*) I know it's a dagger. But I don't use a dagger — apart from the pain have you considered the mess?

Angie I was quoting.

Vincent Quoting. Oh, yes. I suppose you get that from Mr Bryce. Well, it's wasted on me. I left school at fourteen.

Angie I'm sorry — I didn't mean to ——

Vincent That's all right — it's just that I don't like to be rushed.

Angie Of course. I didn't mean to rush you. Let me get you another drink. Sherry?

Vincent Thank you.

Angie (*pouring out two glasses of sherry*) I must say it's nice to know this is being handled by a professional.

Vincent It makes all the difference. How did you hear about Exodus?

Angie A friend told me.

Vincent Yes, we depend a great deal on word of mouth, which is unfortunate since most of our clients aren't talking. We're relatively new in the business but we're expanding rapidly, despite the restrictions on advertising — we still can't get into the Yellow Pages. But we have a computer and a monthly newsletter. We've even tried to organize a few social events but we're never sure who's going to turn up.

Angie smiles

There — I've made you smile. Good. I like to keep things light. To look at me you wouldn't believe I was once an undertaker, would you?

Angie Er, no.

Vincent I was discharged — do you know why? For smiling at the graveside, having a few jokes with the mourners. Of course, they didn't say that; they said it was because I wasn't taking my weight with the coffin, but that wasn't the real reason. They confused dignity with pious solemnity. I mean, why the fuss? We all have to go sometime.

Angie I agree. And if someone's made up her mind, there's no point in arguing about it.

Vincent That's very true.

Angie I think there's a train about twelve.

Vincent Is there? That means I could be in Slough by two — the day wouldn't be completely wasted.

Angie All you have to do is take the cheque and let me have the required dose. The cheque's on the desk — I hope it's satisfactory. (*She crosses to the desk to pick up the cheque*)

Vincent neatly pours the poison into her drink

Vincent Oh yes — more than satisfactory.

Angie Good. (*She hands him the cheque*) Now all you have to do is keep your side of the bargain.

Vincent Of course. Your drink. (*He hands Angie her sherry*) And I must say it's been a pleasure doing business with you. (*He raises his glass*) Here's to the next world, Mrs Bryce.

Angie Oh, I'm not Mrs Bryce.

Vincent (*staring at her*) What?

Walter enters

Angie Walter, you'll never guess what happened. Vincent took me for your wife.

Walter What! (*He knocks the glass from Angie's hand*)

Angie Walter!

Walter turns on Vincent

Vincent Sorry, Mr Bryce.

Walter Sorry! You've only been here half an hour and you've almost killed me and my secretary.

Vincent (*wincing*) Couldn't we put it down to pressure of work?

Walter No, we couldn't!

Angie You mean — you mean — he almost poisoned me? Oh, my God!

She exits into the garden

Walter Angie! (*He goes to follow her. He turns back*) This is professional negligence of the worst possible kind.

Walter exits into the garden

Vincent sighs. He cleans the glass with another tissue, throwing the tissue into the fire. He looks curiously around the room, picking up ornaments and examining them

Celia enters the room. She is in her mid-forties, pale and languid. She wears a flowing negligée

Vincent becomes aware of being watched. He turns

Vincent Hallo. Mrs Bryce?

Celia Yes. Who are you?

Vincent My name's Vincent. I ——

Celia Did my husband send for you?

Vincent Yes.

Celia I thought so. And you think you can help me?

Vincent Well, let's put it this way — I won't have to call again.

Celia You can't dissuade me.

Vincent I wasn't going to.

Celia My mind's made up.

Vincent Splendid.

Celia Please! Don't humour me.

Walter enters

Walter Celia. Oh, I see you've met Vincent.

Celia (*coldly*) Yes.

Walter Er, did he say why he was here?

Celia He didn't have to. I know why he's here. He's a Samaritan, isn't he?

Vincent What?

Walter No, he's not a Samaritan, Celia, but he is here to help you ——

Celia How can he help me? I saw Mother again last night, Walter.

Vincent (*cheerfully*) Oh, and what did she have to say about all this, Mrs Bryce?

Walter (*out of the corner of his mouth*) She's dead.

Vincent Oh, and did she have a message from the other side?

Celia No, she just smiled and beckoned, as she's done many times before.

Vincent And you have this urge to follow?

Celia Yes.

Vincent Then why are you still here?

Celia (*frowning*) Because of Walter. I've stayed for his sake. He's always needed me. He doesn't care how long I suffer.

Walter Well, I've been thinking about that, Celia — and I wonder if I haven't been selfish. I mean, is it fair to you?

Celia (*staring at him*) What?

Walter And Vincent's got this wonderful stuff — it could stop an elephant. It's tasteless, odourless and painless — well, your feet go cold, that's all ——

Celia Walter, what are you talking about? Who is this man?

Walter He's from Exodus.

Celia Exodus!

Vincent You've heard of us. (*Triumphantly*) Our reputation's growing.

Celia Of course I've heard of you. You kill people.

Vincent I don't kill people. I'm a consultant.

Celia (*accusingly*) You want me to die, Walter.

Walter No — I want you to be happy.

Celia But you said you couldn't live without me.

Walter I can't.

Celia You said you could never let me go. That you'd sooner die than lose me.

Walter That's true.

Celia (*staring at him*) Oh, I see. Now I understand.

Walter You do?

Celia You mean — we're going together.

Walter (*after a pause*) What?

Celia That is what you mean ... darling?

Walter (*after a longer pause*) Of course. You don't think I'd let you go alone, do you?

Vincent stares at him in surprise

After all, we go everywhere together.

Celia Walter, you've made me so happy.   KISS.

Walter Good. Unfortunately Vincent has a pressing engagement ... it may mean we'll have to wait. He has to be ——

Vincent (*staring at him*) You mean you're going together? Both of you?

Walter Yes. Didn't I make that clear?

Vincent Not in as many words ... The double. I've never done that before. Mrs Bryce, may I use your phone? I'd like to ring Slough.

Celia Certainly.

Vincent Thank you. (*He picks up the telephone and begins cheerfully to sing "This Is My Lovely Day" from* Bless the Bride)

CURTAIN

SCENE 2

The study/library. Midday

As the CURTAIN *rises, Walter is on the telephone. He glances cautiously over his shoulder*

Walter (*urgently*) Hallo, is that the Samaritans?... This is Walter Bryce, The Martins, Lower Mowbeck. I want you to — what?... Yes. ... Early Georgian. Look, I'd like you to —— it is listed ... yes. Now, I wonder if you could —— the gardens?... Yes, we did open them last year. ... You came?... Good. ... Yes, magnificent. Listen, my wife and I are going to commit suicide before lunch and I want you to come over and stop us. ... What do you mean, oh, no! You're not supposed to? ... Then what are you supposed to do?... Just listen?... Well, that's a fat lot of good. We need restraining. ... The police?... Oh, no. I can't call the police. You must come. You're a Samaritan, aren't you? You're not supposed to

pass by on the other side like the Levite. ... Well, make an exception.
...Your wife's got the car?! ... And then there's lunch. ... Well, yes ... I
know you've got to eat but ... How long have you been doing this job?...
No, I'm not losing my temper. I just want you to come over and talk us
out of it. ... Suppose someone rings while you're away?... Well, I just
hope they have more luck than I'm having. (*He slams the receiver down
and crosses to the rubber plant. He leans forward to examine a leaf more
closely. It comes away in his hand. He groans*)

Angie enters from the garden

Angie Where is she?

Walter She's winding up her affairs.

Angie You mean she's actually going through with it?

Walter Yes, there is one minor complication ——

Angie Where's Vincent?

Walter He's advising her. Apparently he's staying to the bitter end — and
I mean bitter.

Angie That's not a bad thing.

Walter Isn't it?

Angie It serves our purpose even more. If he administers the drug, that
leaves you out of it.

Walter Not entirely.

Angie Of course it does. You won't be giving it to her — he will.

Walter There's one small snag, Angie ——

Angie What's that?

Walter He's giving it to me as well.

Angie What?

Walter She expects me to go with her.

Angie But what made her think that?

Walter She just assumed it. You know what she's like. If she wants to go
somewhere she usually drags me along.

Angie Never mind, Walter. You won't have to put up with it much longer.

Walter No — I'll be dead.

Angie Don't be silly. This is getting better and better.

Walter Are you sure?

Angie Don't you see? How can any suspicion fall on you now?

Walter Of course it won't fall on me — I'll be dead.

Angie You won't be dead.

Walter I won't?

Angie No. You were going to kill youself but at the last moment your nerve failed.

Walter I've got news for you, Angie: I don't have to wait until the last moment — my nerve's failed already.

Angie But you don't have to take the poison.

Walter And if I don't take it what's Celia going to say?

Angie She won't know. Pretend to take it and then palm it.

Walter Palm it? Angie, this is supposed to be a suicide pact. People involved in suicide pacts tend to watch each other rather closely.

Angie Do what Vincent did — pour it on the rubber plant.

Walter I don't think that rubber plant can take much more, Angie. Just look at it. See how limp and bedraggled it's become? That could have been us.

Angie But we can't stop now, we're almost there.

Walter We were almost there an hour ago and it's not an experience I wish to repeat.

Angie All you have to do is take the glass (*she demonstrates with an empty glass*) ... walk across the room ... sigh ... take a last look at the garden ... pass behind the rubber plant ... pour ... and emerge drinking. By which time Celia will probably be in her death throes.

Walter Death throes! He didn't say anything about death throes. He said it would be peaceful. Yes, and what about Vincent? He's set his heart on doing the double and he's running out of patience. He'll be watching me like a cat watches a mouse. If I don't drink he'll probably force it down me through a funnel. He gives me the shivers, Angie. He smells of death.

Angie He smells of something; I'm not sure if it's death — it's more like fried rice.

Walter He lives above a Chinese take-away — not even a restaurant. I think that's what gives him this burning sense of resentment. It's my lifestyle he objects to ... my private education. He left school at fourteen.

Angie I know. He told me.

Walter You see, it's an obsession. He thinks another man's success is his failure.

Angie puts on a cardigan

Where are you going?

Angie Cooper's Bottom.

Walter You're not leaving me?

Angie I can hardly stay, Walter. It would be too macabre, sitting around and watching Celia die. When it's over, come to me there. I'll be waiting.

Walter Angie, I don't know if I can go through with it.

Angie You must. (*softly*) Think of Montego Bay.

Walter Montego Bay. (*He sighs*) I'd almost forgotten ...

They embrace and kiss. A shadow falls across the french windows and grows larger. Angie sees it first

Angie (*formally*) Goodbye, Walter.

Walter What?

Vincent enters

Angie Now I must say goodbye to Celia.

Vincent Are you going, miss?

Angie Yes.

Vincent Will you be coming back when it's over?

Angie Do you think I should?

Vincent I'd appreciate it. You won't find it too disturbing. I'll leave them ... tastefully arranged.

Walter (*wincing*) Tastefully arranged.

Vincent Once you've made the discovery I suggest you call the police.

Angie (*abruptly*) The police?

Walter (*nervously*) The police?

Vincent A mere formality — in the event of sudden death.

Walter Sudden? I thought it was going to be gradual — like falling asleep?

Vincent It is. But any death under suspicious circumstances has to be reported. I suggest you call a doctor as well. You won't get a certificate but he'll be able to pronounce life extinct.

Vincent watches Walter as he wilts under the effect of the following

The police will take care of everything else ... undertakers ... post-mortem ... inquest ... And I'd take it as a personal favour to me if you didn't mention my presence here today. Least said soonest mended. All right?

Angie Of course. I understand. Well, goodbye.
Vincent Goodbye.
Angie Goodbye, Walter. (*She kisses Walter with unexpected warmth*)

She hurries from the room

Vincent (*smiling*) Nice girl.
Walter Yes.

Vincent takes the bottle from his bag and puts it on the drinks tray. He begins to arrange the glasses, whistling cheerfully. He smiles across at Walter, who smiles back weakly

Vincent Not going to change then?
Walter What?
Vincent Happy to go in cords?
Walter Yes. Nothing wrong with cords, is there?
Vincent No. Some people like to dress up, but if you want to keep it informal. (*Pause*) I must say I'm surprised.
Walter Surprised?
Vincent That you made up your mind to go — so unexpectedly ...
Walter Yes, well, I had been thinking about it for some time — I just hadn't come to a decision.
Vincent (*smiling*) I could see you hadn't come to a decision, Mr Bryce. When you thought you might have been poisoned you were running round like a chicken with its head cut off.
Walter It was when I saw how much it meant to my wife.
Vincent Do you do everything your wife wants you to do?
Walter No.

Pause

Vincent Did you know I left school at fourteen, Mr Bryce?
Walter (*softly*) Oh, God.
Vincent I had to make up for my lack of formal education. I took courses. I studied how to increase my word power ... how to win friends and influence people. Memory training. I found that very useful. I have total recall, Mr Bryce. I take everything in at a glance. The holiday brochure on your desk, for example.

Walter (*sharply*) Holiday brochure? (*He crosses to the desk and picks up the brochure*)

Vincent Montego Bay. "Tall and elegant palm trees by shimmering white sands — a turquoise sea and coral reefs with cool green mountains and lush jungle. Sip your piña colada as you take in the sheer beauty and you'll know what they mean by tropical magic." Is that what it says?

Walter (*putting the brochure in the drawer*) Er, yes. I was thinking of taking a holiday before ——

Vincent Before you decided to kill yourself?

Walter Yes.

Vincent Was Mrs Bryce going?

Walter Of course. It was going to be a surprise.

Vincent (*fiercely*) Don't rubbish me, Mr Bryce. I may have left school at fourteen but I'm not a fool. I sensed something was wrong the moment I met your wife. I couldn't help wondering why after all these years of hanging about she'd suddenly decided to go. And I came to the conclusion it wasn't because of the big D. What we have here is the big M — for murder.

Walter No.

Vincent Then why didn't you tell your wife about our little arrangement?

Walter I didn't want to hurt her feelings.

Vincent You're a strange man, Mr Bryce. You'd sooner kill your wife than hurt her feelings.

Walter That's not true.

Vincent When I rang Slough I also checked with the office. You didn't ring them — it was a woman whom they presumed was Mrs Bryce ——

Walter Look, my wife's always wanted to go. We were giving her a gentle push, that's all.

Vincent There's a big difference between a gentle push and a bloody great shove, Mr Bryce. And does Mrs Bryce have timid hopes of immortality?

Walter Yes, I believe so.

Vincent Well, she's going to be very disappointed when she looks round and finds you're not there. And where will you be? Stretched out in Montego Bay sipping your piña colada. Listen, if you want to bump her off that's your affair, but why involve me?

Walter I don't want to bump her off.

Vincent No — you want me to do it. You don't need me. It's open season on wives these days. Judges can be very lenient. Say she boasted of her infidelity and you killed her.

Walter But she's never been unfaithful.
Vincent (*staring at him*) Never?
Walter No.
Vincent She must be a very unusual woman.
Walter She is. And I don't want to kill her. I just want to be free.
Vincent Then why stay? Look at those doors. Notice anything? The bolts are on the inside. There are no bars at the windows. There's nothing to keep you here. You could be as free as a bird.
Walter You don't understand. She's very sensitive ... easily hurt. If I were to leave now she'd probably kill herself ——

Silence as they both realize what Walter has said

Vincent What was that, Mr Bryce?
Walter (*lamely*) I mean, I couldn't hurt her like that.
Vincent You mean, she's got the money.
Walter Well, yes. There's not much money in literature these days.
Vincent I see. And you expect me to endanger my professional reputation because there's no money in literature?
Walter I'm sorry.
Vincent Your cheque is on the desk, Mr Bryce. Tear it up.
Walter Certainly. (*He tears up the cheque*) Look, Vincent, I'm sorry. I don't know what came over me. It must have been the strain of these last few weeks. Let's forget the whole thing.
Vincent Make out another one.
Walter What?
Vincent Another cheque — for five thousand.
Walter Five thousand!?
Vincent I said the fee was flexible, didn't I?
Walter Yes.
Vincent Well, I've just thought of a firm price. Take it or leave it.
Walter But five thousand ——
Vincent Is my reputation worth less?
Walter No, I suppose not.
Vincent Just fill in the amount and sign it. I'll add the other details later.
Walter (*writing out the cheque*) There's just one thing that worries me.
Vincent What's that?
Walter My wife thinks we're going together. How do we make sure I don't get the poison?

Vincent Don't worry. We'll put two glasses on this tray. I'll mask the tray with my body.

Walter But ——

Vincent You didn't see me put it in last time, did you?

Walter No.

Vincent I'll simply slip my little herbal remedy into her drink and leave yours alone.

Walter Yes. Don't think I'm being fussy, but wouldn't it be better if the glasses were different? If I were to drink from the red goblet?

Vincent Do you normally drink from the red goblet?

Walter Well, no ...

Vincent Mr Bryce, if we give you the red goblet, don't you think your wife's going to be suspicious?

Walter I don't know ...

Vincent If you were taking part in a suicide pact and your partner suddenly produced a red goblet he's never drunk from before, wouldn't it raise a question mark? (*He holds up the red goblet and compares it to a cocktail glass*)

Walter I suppose so.

Vincent The important thing is not to arouse suspicion.

Walter But you will be careful.

Vincent Careful is my middle name, Mr Bryce.

Walter You haven't been very careful up to now.

Vincent (*frowning*) That's something I've noticed about you. The way you keep throwing people's mistakes in their faces. All right, I made a boo-boo, but that's behind us now. (*Brightly*) What's your poison?

Walter Pardon?

Vincent What do you normally drink at this time of day?

Walter A dry martini.

Vincent Good.

Walter Good?

Vincent It goes very well with a dry martini. (*He begins mixing the drinks*) Now, would you summon your wife, Mr Bryce.

Walter exits reluctantly

Vincent shakes the martinis and sings "This Is My Lovely Day" again

Withers enters abruptly from the hall. He is an intense-looking man. He goes to Vincent and takes his arm

Withers Thank God I'm not too late.

Vincent What?

Withers I borrowed a car and came the back way. I thought time was of the essence. That's why I didn't ring the doorbell — I hope you don't mind.

Vincent (*cautiously*) Not at all.

Withers Fortunately I knew the house. You realize I shouldn't even be here.

Vincent Where should you be?

Withers Manning the phone. You know who I am?

Vincent No — who are you?

Withers My name's Withers — oh, damn — I shouldn't have told you that. We're not supposed to reveal our identity.

Vincent Who's we?

Withers I'm the Samaritan.

Vincent Samaritan!

Withers You rang me a short while ago. (*He sighs*) Please, don't have any more to drink, Mr Bryce. Come here, let me look at you.

He draws Vincent to the sofa

Yes ... I can see you're emotionally disturbed.

Vincent What?!

Withers (*taking Vincent's hand*) Well, I'm not going to let go of this hand until I've talked you out of this whole wretched business. Honestly, I could give you a good shaking.

Vincent Could you?

Withers Here you are ... a scholar ... intellect ... man of letters ... surrounded by the wisdom of the ages and yet you're contemplating an act that the beasts of the field would scorn to consider.

Vincent The beasts of the field!

Withers Animals don't commit suicide, Mr Bryce.

Vincent No, but then they don't write books, do they? What's more — they don't have to read them. They don't have to go on package holidays to Benidorm, or take out a ninety-nine per cent mortgage on a Georgian semi. They don't have to sit for four hours every day on the M25. And they don't have to watch *Panorama* or *News at Ten*. In fact, they lead untroubled lives — why should they commit suicide?

Withers I suppose I should have expected this sophistry from a writer.

Vincent This what?

Withers Do you think that being a writer makes you different from the rest of us?

Vincent Of course it does. We feel things more, don't we? We have to peel back the layers — strip our emotions bare. I'm too sensitive, too highly tuned — that's my trouble.

Withers Because you have to empathize?

Vincent (*after a pause*) That as well.

Withers But it's not your life to take, Mr Bryce.

Vincent Then whose is it?

Withers Dare I say ... God's?

Vincent Dare I say ... codswallop?

Withers What?

Vincent He's never shown any interest in my life before.

Withers How can you say that when you're surrounded by all this? You have a lot to be thankful for, Mr Bryce.

Vincent And do you have a lot to be thankful for, Mr Withers?

Withers Indeed. I have a house by the river ... four wonderful children ... and a perfect wife.

Vincent Then you're lucky.

Withers We're all lucky, Mr Bryce. It's a wonderful world.

Vincent Is it?

Withers The sun's shining ... it's a perfect day.

Vincent Look again, Mr Withers. There's a cloud no bigger than a man's fist but it's growing — there'll be rain before tea.

Withers But it hasn't rained in weeks.

Vincent That's the greenhouse effect due to the destruction of the rain forests ... the burning of fossil fuels and toxic waste. We've damaged the ozone layer and it's beyond repair.

Withers (*nervously*) Well, hardly that ...

Vincent Did you know that in Tokyo you can't cross the street without an oxygen mask? No wonder hari-kari seems such an attractive proposition to those people — they'd keep you busy there, Mr Withers. Then there's radiation and acid rain. And what about the ice cap?

Withers (*worried*) What about the ice cap?

Vincent It's going to melt. And where will you be then?

Withers I don't know. (*He slowly lets go of Vincent's hand*)

Vincent In a mess. Because the Thames Valley's going to be under twenty feet of water and that'll play havoc with property values — particularly yours. (*He smiles*) You've let go of my hand, Mr Withers.

Withers I'm sorry, Mr Bryce. I'm confused. You don't sound like the man on the phone, pleading for help.

Vincent I'm extremely volatile.

Withers Perhaps I'm wasting my time — I am extremely busy.

Vincent A lot of work on at the moment?

Withers I'm afraid so. Small businessmen mainly but I do have a pressing problem at Slough.

Vincent Slough!

Withers Yes, he's been on the phone constantly. University lecturer — on the brink.

Vincent You can't blame him, living in Slough. I mean, that's worse than Maidenhead, that is.

Withers (*puzzled*) Is it?

Vincent "Come friendly bombs and fall on Slough." That's what I always say.

Withers Yes ... Perhaps I'd better get back — he may ring.

Vincent But I thought you were going to dissuade me?

Withers (*hesitating*) Is it your wife?

Vincent How did you guess?

Withers It usually is. Has she been unfaithful?

Vincent (*broodingly*) Yes. She had a long standing affair with a stoker off H.M.S. Belfast.

Withers (*gaping*) Your wife and a stoker — I can hardly believe it!

Vincent Neither could I ... Mind you, she's always had a weakness for sailors. Still, it was a bit of a shock. It came out of a clear blue sky, Mr Withers.

Withers Didn't you suspect anything?

Vincent Suspect? Let me ask you something: do you know where your wife is at the moment?

Withers Well, yes. ~~She's taken the children to Mother's and then she's~~ gone off to see an old school friend in Windsor.

Vincent Windsor.

Withers What's the matter?

Vincent That's worse than Slough, that is. The sights I've seen in those streets — even with the Royal Family in residence. Windsor.

Withers Mr Bryce ——

Vincent And have you met this old school friend?

Withers Well, not for years.

Vincent Oh.

Withers Our paths don't normally cross. What are you suggesting?

Vincent I see a cloud no bigger than a man's fist, Mr Withers. Perhaps the first glimpse of the canker on the rose.

Withers Mr Bryce, I didn't come here to discuss my wife. I came because for once I wanted to reach out to that disembodied voice ... to reach out and help.

Vincent And you have.

Withers What?

Vincent (*beaming*) You've lightened my mood considerably. That comes from talking to an optimist. Someone who believes in life, with faith and certainty.

Withers (*uncertainly*) Yes.

Vincent Congratulations, Mr Withers. You've triumphed.

Withers I have?

Vincent I'm not going to do it. Look at me — I'm smiling. I haven't done that for six weeks.

He guides Withers to the french windows

I can't thank you enough. You can make your way out through the garden ...

Withers pauses uncertainly

Oh, and don't worry about Windsor. Probably nothing to it. And keep smiling — it's a wonderful world ...

Withers exits, looking worried and uncertain. Walter enters

Vincent turns from the window

Walter She's not ready yet. That woman would be late for her own funeral. (*He winces*) Why did I have to say that.

Vincent I'll fetch her, Mr Bryce. I'd like another word with her — put her in the right frame of mind.

Vincent exits

Walter crosses to the drinks tray

Withers (*off*) Psst!

Walter turns

Withers enters through the french windows

Walter Who're you?
Withers My name's Withers. Damn! I shouldn't have told you that.
Walter Are you the Samaritan?
Withers Yes.

Walter closes the interior door

Walter My wife mustn't know you're here. She'd never forgive me.
Withers Then you are Mr Bryce?
Walter Yes.
Withers I thought so. Then who was that strange man?
Walter (*hysterically*) You think he's strange, we could've had Peaseblossom. Did you smell the fried rice? Lives above a take-away. You didn't tell him who you were? He'd kill me if he found out — he'll probably kill me anyway — just to keep his eye in.
Withers Mr Bryce, take a grip of yourself. Who is he?
Walter He's from Exodus.
Withers (*appalled*) You sent for Exodus?
Walter Er, no, my wife did.
Withers Then you're both in grave danger.
Walter Please, don't say grave. I've already had one brush with death. It was awful. You must help me.
Withers Then I must speak with your wife.
Walter You can't. She mustn't know you're here.
Withers Then I don't see how I can help you.
Walter Tell me what to say. How to talk her out of it.
Withers (*after a pause*) It's a wonderful world, Mr Bryce.
Walter I know it's a wonderful world but she thinks it's five minutes to midnight.
Withers Then hold her and tell her you love her.
Walter (*staring at him*) Do you think that'll help?

Withers It may. But first I must know something. Has she had an affair?

Walter An affair?

Withers With a stoker from H.M.S. Belfast?

Walter Certainly not! What made you say a disgusting thing like that?

Withers Sorry. I'm simply trying to ascertain the facts. If I'm to help I need to know everything. Do you have any children?

Walter No.

Withers Ah.

Walter What do you mean, ah? Do you?

Withers We have four.

Walter Oh.

Withers My wife and I have a very good relationship.

Walter You must do with four children.

Withers And do you have a good relationship, Mr Bryce?

Walter Isn't this getting rather personal?

Withers I'm afraid I must ask these questions if I'm to help. When did your wife first reveal these suicidal tendencies?

Walter On our honeymoon.

Withers Ah.

Walter What do you mean, ah?

Withers That must have cast quite a cloud over the proceedings.

Walter It did. She threatened to jump from Beachy Head.

Withers How disturbing.

Walter Yes — she was holding my hand at the time.

Withers Did something happen? Did she see, or experience, something so shocking that she preferred to jump off Beachy Head sooner than face it a second time?

Walter (*indignantly*) No! She's always threatening things like that. Last week we were out in the car ... She was driving at about ninety miles an hour and she suddenly said, I feel like running this car into a brick wall.

Withers What did you say?

Walter I said, do you mind if I get out first?

Withers That wasn't very sympathetic.

Walter I wasn't feeling very sympathetic. You don't know what it's like being married to someone who's weary of the world. It can be very depressing. And why does she always have to involve me?

Withers Mr Bryce, I could give you a good shaking. Don't you see these are cries for help? (*Pause*) Do you really love your wife?

Walter (*cautiously*) Do you love yours?

Withers Yes.

Walter Well, so do I.

Withers Then you must show it — in every way.

Walter Every way?

Withers Every way, Mr Bryce. This morning when I awoke I picked a rose covered in dew and laid it upon my wife's pillow while she slept.

Walter (*impressed*) Did you really?

Withers On our fifteenth wedding anniversary we made love on our garden seat.

Walter You must have very understanding neighbours.

Withers It was midnight, Mr Bryce — in January. We've kept our marriage alive and you must do the same. You must put excitement back into your lives. Never take each other for granted. Look for the danger signs. Boredom. Restlessness. Windsor.

Walter Windsor?

Withers Pardon?

Walter You said Windsor.

Withers Did I? (*He glances at his watch*) I must leave you now, Mr Bryce. I have things to do.

Walter But what am I supposed to do?

Withers You must delay, Mr Bryce. At all costs delay. Do everything to postpone the event. If we can dissuade her from taking this fatal step today — then perhaps tomorrow things will look different. I'll be in touch. (*He pauses by the french windows. Uncertainly*) Remember — it's a wonderful world.

Withers exits

~~Walter starts to pour himself a drink, then thinks better of it and doesn't~~ Goes to fireplace

Celia enters with Vincent. She is tastefully dressed and looking radiant

Walter Celia!

Celia What?

Walter You look wonderful.

Celia Thank you. Is everything ready?

Walter Ready? Oh, I though you may have changed your mind.

Celia No, why should I change my mind?

Walter I didn't realize you were going to dress up. Would you like me to change? It's no trouble.

Celia No, it's too late for that, Walter.

Vincent (*cheerfully*) Dry martini, Mrs Bryce?

Celia Thank you.

Vincent Good. (*He flourishes the cocktail shaker*) The advantage of
alcohol is that it speeds up the assimilation into the blood stream. (*He
pours the drinks*)

Walter Speeds up? We're not in any hurry, are we?

~~**Vincent** Ice?~~

~~**Celia** Thank you.~~

Vincent Twist of lemon?

Celia Yes, we always have lemon.

Vincent I wouldn't drink it any other way.

Walter Wait a minute. How do we know it's painless? We could die in
agony, and a twist of lemon's not going to help.

Celia Well, what do you suggest, Walter?

Walter (*hesitating*) Couldn't we try it on the dog?

Celia (*shocked*) The dog!

Vincent The dog! I didn't come here to destroy the dog, Mr Bryce. And
there won't be any agony. Just a cold sensation rising up the limbs ...
gradual paralysis ... a feeling of dizziness ... blurred vision ——

Walter You didn't say anything about paralysis and blurred vision ——

Vincent — and when it reaches the heart, that's it.

Walter That's it.

Vincent If you walk around it'll take no time at all.

Walter I think we'll sit.

Celia Yes. Come and sit by me, Walter. Vincent, would you bring the
drinks over here?

Vincent Certainly. (*He places the drinks on the coffee table*)

Walter (*peering suspiciously*) Which is mine?

Celia But, darling, they're both the same. There's no difference, is there?

Walter No, of course not.

Celia Relax, Walter. Take my hand. Look at the garden — isn't it lovely?
I'm glad we waited for the tulips.

Walter Yes. (*Pause*) Pity about the lawns.

Celia What?

Walter They could do with a cut. It's just a thought, but is there time to
get the mower out?

Celia Of course not. Vincent has to get to Slough. Should we drink?

Vincent In your own time, Mrs Bryce.

Celia You know what this reminds me of, Walter? Our wedding day.

Walter (*staring at her*) What?

Celia Hand in hand into the unknown.

Walter (*under his breath*) God.

Celia Ready then, Walter? (*She raises her glass*)

Walter Wait a minute. I feel like a cigarette.

Celia (*staring at him*) But you don't smoke.

Walter And do you know why? I always thought it would be bad for my health.

Vincent That's all right, Mr Bryce. I usually carry some for these occasions. (*He hands him a cigarette*) Low tar. (*He lights the cigarette*) Take your time. No rush.

Celia Well, whilst Walter's smoking his first cigarette—is there anything we may have forgotten, Vincent?

Vincent There is one thing — disposal of the remains.

Walter chokes on his cigarette

It is a good thing to leave definite instructions.

Celia Oh yes, I've seen to that. We're going to be cremated.

Walter (*stubbing his cigarette out with great deliberation*) I don't want to be cremated.

Celia You don't?

Walter No.

Celia But you've always wanted to be cremated.

Walter I've changed my mind.

Celia But our ashes were going to be sprinkled into the stream at the bottom of the garden ... the stream would flow into the river ... the river into the sea ... and the sea into the oceans.

Vincent (*smiling*) That should appeal to you, Mr Bryce, with your tidal view of humanity.

Walter Well, it doesn't. I don't want to go from stream to river ... from river to sea ... from sea to ocean. I want to go from the soil to plants ... from plants to food ... from food to people.

Celia That's a very strange idea, Walter.

Vincent That's the nitrogen cycle. Is that your idea of the next life, Mr Bryce — coming back as a sliced loaf?

Walter I'm sorry, Celia. We just haven't thought this one out. I don't want to be cremated and that's final.

Celia I wish you'd said so before. This is most inconsiderate.

Vincent Perhaps I could say something, Mrs Bryce. I left school at fourteen but since then I've studied most of the religions of the world. You name it. Catholicism, Protestantism, Calvinism, Buddhism, Hinduism, Shintoism. Also Transmigration, Reincarnation, Meditation and Levitation. I've done the lot. And I've come to one firm conclusion.

Celia What's that?

Vincent When you're dead you're dead.

Celia Oh. Well, perhaps I'm making too much fuss, Vincent. Would you inform Angie that Walter has expressed a preference for interment, and to make the necessary arrangements?

Vincent Certainly.

Celia Now perhaps we can get on. (*She looks at Walter and sighs*) What's the matter now, Walter?

Walter Just supposing, Celia — and this is pure supposition — that there is a God and he's a fierce old man in flowing robes and a long white beard ...

Celia Yes?

Walter Well, he's not going to be very pleased with us, Celia — throwing this sacred gift back in his face.

Celia But Walter, you don't believe in God. You're an atheist.

Walter No, I'm an agnostic. There's a difference. Let me explain ——

Vincent (*snarling*) Mr Bryce, are we going to do this or not?

Walter (*hesitating*) Well, yes ... but ...

Vincent Then should we get this show on the road?

Celia Hold my hand. I know you're afraid, darling, but don't be. I'll be with you. Now say something lovely to me because these will be the last words we'll speak to each other.

Walter Celia ...

Celia Yes?

Walter Don't drink — it's poisoned!

Celia I know that. I thought you might have said you love me.

Walter I love you.

Celia Is that all?

Walter Celia, you're going to die.

Celia I know I'm going to die. Don't be obvious, darling. Kiss me.

They kiss. Celia picks up a glass and drinks

Walter You drank it.

Celia Yes.

Walter My poor Celia ... (*He looks down*) Was that your glass?

Celia What's the difference?

Walter What?

Celia Drink, Walter. *Raises glass*

Walter (*hesitating*) What was it like?

Celia A little bitter, that was all.

Walter (*hopefully*) Bitter?

Celia Drink, my love.

Walter Yes.

Walter looks at Vincent, who smiles reassuringly. Walter sips his drink cautiously

Celia (*firmly*) Deeper.

Walter drinks deeper. He regards Celia

Walter (*anxiously*) How do you feel?

Celia (*rising*) I feel wonderful. If this is dying, why are we so afraid? There's no pain.

Walter How are your feet, Celia?

Celia Winged. I'm running to a safe haven. My head is clear ... my eye is bright ...

Walter No dizziness?

Celia No — just elation.

Walter No coldness rising up the legs?

Celia All I feel is a sense of wellbeing. (*She extends her hand*) Come, Walter — walk with me as far as the trees ...

Walter half rises and stops, petrified

Walter I can't! It's my legs. They've gone cold. I can't move them. My God! I've been poisoned.

Celia Of course, you've been poisoned, Walter. If you can't walk — one last embrace.

Walter Poisoned! Why did I let you talk me into this, you ridiculous woman.

Celia Walter, don't rave and shout — not at a time like this.

Walter But I'm dying, you stupid cow.

Celia (*shocked*) Walter.

Vincent You're not dying, Mr Bryce.

Walter Of course I am. Allow me to be the judge of whether I'm dying or not.

Vincent You can't be.

Walter I drank the poison.

Vincent No, you didn't. There wasn't any.

Walter What?

Celia You mean we aren't going to die?

Vincent No. What Mr Bryce is experiencing is the placebo effect. There's nothing wrong with him.

Walter (*moving his legs cautiously*) He's right. I can move them. (*Excitedly*) I'm going to be all right. I'm going to live. I'm going to —— (*He catches Celia's eye and stops*) Damn it, Vincent, this isn't good enough. After all we've been through you have the nerve to tell us there wasn't any poison? I'll certainly have something to say about this.

Celia Are you trying to make fools of us, Vincent?

Vincent No, Mrs Bryce.

Celia But you can hardly call this responsible professional behaviour.

Vincent On the contrary, I was exercising my professional discretion, Mrs Bryce. When I came here today I almost made a dreadful mistake — two dreadful mistakes. A fact that has been constantly drawn to my attention. I couldn't afford a third. I had to be sure. And to say I had misgivings is putting it mildly.

Celia Misgivings?

Vincent And when we have misgivings our instructions are clear. We must give the client an opportunity to change his or her mind. What we have here is a cooling off period. After all, you get that with an H.P. agreement and that's far less binding.

Celia A cooling off period! I'd like to point out, Vincent, that had you done your job properly we'd have both been cooling off quite nicely by now.

Walter That's right.

Celia Now we have to go through the whole thing again.

Walter (*gaping*) What?

Vincent You mean you still intend to go through with it?

Celia Surely you can't doubt the seriousness of our intentions after what happened?

Vincent Well, I don't doubt yours but what about Mr Bryce? He did give his now familiar impression of a scalded cat.

Celia He panicked, that was all. He's always had a nervous disposition. Now, I suggest we start again after lunch.

Vincent After lunch?

Walter I don't feel like any lunch ...

Celia There — you see what you've done? He normally has a wonderful appetite.

Walter (*faintly*) I think I'll go and lie down.

Walter exits

Celia Yes, you do that, Walter. Just leave everything to us ...

Celia and Vincent regard each other in silence and then smile. There is an air of conspiracy LONG PAUSE

Vincent Well, Mrs Bryce?

Celia (*thoughtfully*) Yes ... you were right, Vincent.

Vincent His heart's not really in it, is it?

Celia I had noticed that.

Vincent Well, no harm done. (*He picks up his coat and bag*) And I think he's learned his lesson.

Celia You're not going?

Vincent I must get to Slough.

Celia But what about this afternoon?

Vincent (*surprised*) You're not still going through with it, Mrs Bryce?

Celia But of course. Why don't you stay here while I fix a spot of lunch. I have some excellent cold ham.

Vincent Cold ham. (*He smiles*) That would be delightful, Mrs Bryce.

Celia Why don't you read a book — there's plenty to choose from.

Vincent Yes ... (*He looks at the bookcase*)

Celia Anything I can find for you?

Vincent Do you have anything on ... Crippen?

CURTAIN

ACT II
Scene 1

The same. Mid-afternoon

The sun no longer streams through the windows and the day has become overcast. The rubber plant has turned yellow and has lost several of its leaves

As the Curtain *rises, Walter is on the telephone*

Walter (*urgently*) The Samaritans?... Is that you, Withers?... He's gone out?... (*He sighs*) Look, I know it's you, Withers — so don't try and disguise your voice. This is Walter Bryce — my wife and I were going to kill ourselves before lunch, but we didn't? ... Well, of course we didn't or I wouldn't be ringing you, would I? ... No, I'm not losing my temper. ... Yes, I know it's a wonderful world. I simply want to say I've delayed things as much as possible and there's nothing else I can do. If anything happens now, it's on your head, Withers.

Celia enters

Er, I'll ring you back later. Goodbye. (*He hangs up*)
Celia (*regarding him curiously*) Who was that, Walter?
Walter (*quickly*) The hospital.
Celia Hospital?
Walter Yes. I thought I'd donate my organs — I mean, I won't have much use for them after today.
Celia And which organs precisely were you thinking of donating, Walter?
Walter Oh, the usual ... heart, liver, kidneys.
Celia Do you think they'd be any good to them? After all, they've taken a fair amount of punishment these last few years — particularly the liver. And as for the heart, I thought it was going to pack up before lunch.
Walter I thought it might be worth a try — it would be nice to think some part of me was still getting around when I was dead and gone. (*Musing*) Perhaps if we'd had children.

Celia (*staring at him*) Children?

Walter I haven't mentioned this before but did you know I'm the last of the Bryces?

Celia ~~No, I didn't know that.~~ Mmmm

Walter Yes ... Sad to think that when I die the name of Bryce is going to die with me.

Celia I'm sure you'll find plenty in the phone book, Walter. And they won't accept your organs — they'll be reserved for the autopsy.

Walter (*wincing*) It was just a thought. (*He rises*)

Celia Where are you going?

Walter I thought I'd take a walk around the garden.

Celia Well, don't be too long. And put your coat on, it looks like rain. We don't want you to catch a chill ——

Walter gives her a long-suffering look and exits through the french windows

Celia watches him through the glass

Vincent enters

I'm afraid Walter's delaying us again. He now has a sudden desire to breed. I said you can't possibly wait that long.

Vincent I see. Well, there is a solution if he cares to trust me in the matter. It would mean a codicil in the will, of course.

Celia What's that?

Vincent We could take his seed and keep it frozen — it would mean time and trouble but it would get us out of this particular situation.

Celia (*staring at him*) Take his seed and what?

Vincent Keep it in a freezer. Until a surrogate mother can be found.

Celia No, I don't think so, Vincent.

Vincent Perhaps you're right. It's not a very reliable method. Someone's only got to leave the door open and you lose your son and heir along with the kippers. The truth is, Mr Bryce seems too full of the life force to be thinking of death.

Celia Yes. Are you a married man, Vincent?

Vincent I was.

Celia Oh, what happened?

Vincent It didn't work out. I got rid of her.

Celia (*shocked*) You don't mean ——
Vincent Oh, no. Divorce. (*Darkly*) Mind you, that would have been
  cheaper.
Celia Oh. Well, then, perhaps you can understand that my own marriage
  has been less than perfect. I stayed with Walter because he needed me
  desperately. He loves me deeply.
Vincent I wouldn't depend on that, Mrs Bryce.
Celia I don't. He depends on me. Life would hold nothing for Walter if
  I were to die ... So you see ...(*she returns to the window*) it would almost
  be a kindness to take him with me ...
Vincent Are you sure? Perhaps his life has taken on a new dimension
  recently.
Celia You don't know my husband.
Vincent Do you, Mrs Bryce?
Celia Oh, I can't say I wasn't hurt when you told me he had no intention
  of taking the poison. That's why I agreed to our little charade. I had to
  see if he'd go through with it. And when it finally came down to it, he
  couldn't. You saw what happened. He tried to prevent it.
Vincent With respect, Mrs Bryce, he wasn't sure if he had the right glass.
  What you saw was his instinct for self-preservation.
Celia Nonsense. He changed his mind. At the last moment he couldn't
  face life without me. And do you know why? Because he'd find it empty
  and drab.
Vincent Empty and drab! He's taking delivery of a new car next week.
Celia What?
Vincent You'll find the details in the drawer — top right hand.

Celia looks in the desk drawer

  And he hasn't got it for the funeral — it's in terracotta red.
Celia (*uncertainly*) Well, that doesn't mean anything. Walter loves cars
  — he always has one on order.
Vincent And why is he so deep into holiday literature?
Celia What?
Vincent Keep looking, Mrs Bryce. You'll see he's also planning a trip to
  Montego Bay — a strange place to choose for a period of mourning,
  wouldn't you agree?
Celia That doesn't prove anything. He clearly intended to surprise me. He
  wouldn't have gone alone. We're inseparable — we go everywhere
  together.

Vincent Everywhere except Cooper's Bottom.

Celia (*staring at him*) Cooper's Bottom? I don't understand.

Vincent That's where they meet.

Celia Who?

Vincent Mr Bryce and his secretary.

Celia What are you talking about?

Vincent They're having an affair, Mrs Bryce.

Celia Having an affair? That's ridiculous. Angie's the daughter of one of my closest friends. I had to persuade Walter to take her on. What on earth makes you think they're having an affair?

Vincent I sensed it, Mrs Bryce. I sensed it the moment I entered this house.

Celia How dare you. How dare you sense things in my house. Walter's not having an affair. Angie's years younger than he is.

Vincent Be that as it may, they have a way of looking at each other that makes me think this whole business has been an elaborate conspiracy to eliminate you, Mrs Bryce.

Celia Eliminate me?

Vincent Now, if you don't mind I'll leave before someone gets hurt.

Celia No.

Vincent Call it off, Mrs Bryce.

Celia (*emotionally*) Call it off! Do you think I'd want to live if what you say is true? If I had reason to kill myself before I have double the reason now. But I don't believe you. Walter loves me and he'd never let me go. He's proved it time and again ——

Vincent Do you know how much your death is worth to him? (*He shows her the cheque*)

Celia Five thousand —— (*She tears the cheque into tiny fragments and crosses to the door*)

Vincent Where are you going?

Celia To my room.

Vincent You won't do anything ... silly.

They both realize what he's said

She gives him a withering stare and exits

Mrs Bryce ...

Vincent follows her out. Walter enters from the garden.

He pours a drink, sighs, and then crosses and stretches out on the sofa. He closes his eyes

Angie enters and looks around anxiously

She sees Walter, but hesitates to touch him. She sees the glass on the table beside him and sniffs at it. She bends over Walter and listens. She touches him gingerly with her finger. He groans. She places her hand over his heart and bears down savagely. He yelps. She recoils

Walter My God! What are you doing?

Angie Walter! I thought you were dying.

Walter Well, couldn't you have given me the kiss of life? That hurt.

Angie I'm sorry. But I waited and waited and you didn't come — and when I saw you stretched out there — I thought there'd been a dreadful mistake.

Walter There nearly was, Angie.

Angie Did she go through with it?

Walter Oh yes, she went through with it. It was a nightmare.

Angie Never mind — it's all over now.

Walter It certainly is. I couldn't go through that again.

Angie Where is she?

Walter In her room.

Angie Good. I'm glad she's not here. I want to remember her as she was.

Walter What?

Angie Tall and beautiful. And she was beautiful, in her own way. Well, perhaps more attractive than beautiful ——

Walter Angie, I think there's something I should tell you ——

Angie We must try and remember the good things about her, Walter. And there were good things. Her kindness to animals. Remember the squirrel with the broken leg?

Walter She's not dead, Angie.

Angie (*staring at him*) You mean the cow didn't go through with it after all?

Walter No.

Angie (*accusingly*) You talked her out of it.

Walter No, I didn't. I thought I wouldn't have the nerve but I did. There was a lot of tension in here, Angie. But I was impassive and I went through with it. But that raving lunatic hadn't put the poison in. Now she wants to go through with it all over again. Of course, it's out of the question.

Angie Why is it out of the question?

Walter She's not going to die, Angie.

Angie No, it's the people around her who begin to die.

Walter (*with a sigh*) Yes. Even the squirrel turned its toes up. I remember the day it died. I could see by her face that something was wrong; she has this expression for death. It steals over her face like a frost. She said, "Nutkin's gone." I felt one day she'll be looking down at me like that. "Walter's gone."

Angie No, she won't, Walter, because we're going through with it.

Walter We can't. Vincent knows everything. He's demanding money.

Angie Then pay him. Where is he?

Walter He's talking to Celia.

Angie Again? They seem to find an awful lot to talk about. I'll try and speak to him alone. You rest. You look worn out.

She exits

Walter slumps back on to the sofa and closes his eyes

Withers enters stealthily through the french windows and observes Walter

He leans over and listens to Walter's heart. He abruptly pushes Walter's head back, forces his mouth open and pinches his nose in preparation for the kiss of life

Walter (*sitting up; in indignant nasal tones*) What do you think you're playing at?

Withers I'm sorry, Mr Bryce. I thought you'd finally done it.

Walter Well, I haven't.

Withers And your wife?

Walter No, she hasn't done it either.

Withers Good. I think we're winning. Did you talk her out of it — did she have second thoughts?

Walter Oh no — she downed it like nobody's business, but unfortunately there was nothing in her glass.

Withers (*staring at him*) Unfortunately?

Walter What?

Withers You said unfortunately.

Walter I meant fortunately.

Withers Did you? Or was that a Freudian slip?

Walter Don't analyse me, Withers.

Withers Do you secretly hate your wife, Mr Bryce?

Walter Certainly not. Only she's a very difficult woman. She keeps saying, "What does it all mean — what's the point of it all — what's it all about?" Well, I don't know and it can be very depressing.

Withers You're depressed — my wife's not in Windsor.

Walter Windsor?

Withers Of course, there's a point. Look out there at nature ... all that beauty. That didn't happen by accident — it has purpose and pattern. It was created by a superior intelligence.

Walter Yes. The gardener.

Withers But who directs the gardener's hand?

Walter She does.

Withers You miss the point. Mrs Bryce is always looking beyond for the answer but this could be our Heaven, right here and now.

Walter We're in Heaven?

Withers Yes.

Walter If we're in Heaven, we're dead already, so what's the fuss about?

Withers I mean this could be our paradise if we made it so. All we need is love. Did you tell your wife that you love her?

Walter Yes, well, I did try and squeeze it into the conversation.

Withers Squeeze it in! I'm going to be brutally frank, Mr Bryce. When did you and your wife last have fulfilment?

Walter Fulfilment?

Withers Yes.

Walter I think this is getting personal again, Withers.

Withers I must know.

Walter She does have a bad back. I carelessly erected a deckchair one day and it collapsed. She's never forgiven me.

Withers So?

Walter Well, it makes fulfilment on the garden seat out of the question. And we're not demonstrative. No dewy roses, that sort of thing ...

Withers When, Mr Bryce?

Walter I don't recall exactly. I don't think I'm prepared to discuss this.

Withers Does your wife find the idea objectionable?

Walter No. She has a sort of flag day approach to it.

Withers Flag day?

Walter Well, if it's in a good cause and not too often, she doesn't mind giving.

Withers I think we've come to the root of the problem. Can't you see what's happened? It's staring you in the face. You've fallen out of love. The romance has gone out of your marriage. That's why she sent for this man. You don't excite her anymore, Mr Bryce. You must fight for your wife's love, just as I shall fight for mine.

Walter (*staring at him*) Yours?

Withers Don't listen to him. He corrodes everything he touches — he poisons everything.

Walter Actually, he hasn't poisoned anything yet — except the rubber plant.

Withers We'll defeat him, Mr Bryce, together. He won't have his shabby triumph here. We're going to let in the sun ... affirm our belief in life and happiness. I must speak to your wife.

Walter You can't. If she finds out who you are, she'll never forgive me.

Withers Then don't tell her. (*He begins tucking his trousers into his socks*)

Walter What are you doing?

Withers Tell her I'm merely a passing cyclist who called for a drink of water, and you invited me in to partake of ... of an orange juice. (*He pours out a glass of orange juice*) Call her, Mr Bryce, and trust me. You're in safe hands.

Walter (*wearily*) I think I've heard that before.

Walter exits

Withers sips his orange juice. He picks up the telephone and dials

Withers (*into the phone*) Ah! Home at last. And where have you been?... Of course it's me. Who were you expecting?... I'm not checking up on you. I just wondered if you'd picked up your children. ... There's nothing wrong. ... Only I rang Victoria Swayfield earlier — she hasn't seen you in ten years. What do you say to that, you tart?... Miranda Pulfrey?... Oh. ... But I always thought it was Veronica Swayfield. ... Miranda. Fancy that. ... Called you what?... No, sweetheart. Must have been the line. How is dear Miranda?... Good. I'll see you later. ... Bye, darling. (*He hangs up. He frowns*) Who the hell's Miranda Pulfrey? (*He picks up the phone and dials again*) Hallo, Slough? My name's Withers — blast. I thought we should keep in touch. ... Still there, anyway. ... Only just? Well, hang on, I implore you. ... Exodus! No, I'm not from Exodus. I'm a Samaritan. I wish you'd make up your mind which service you require. ... Look, it's a wonderful world. ... Not from where you're standing?... Well, mine's not exactly a bed of roses. ... You've got problems? We've all got problems. ... So your wife's been unfaithful. I don't see why that should surprise you. All women are faithless. ... I'm not losing my temper. ... Don't ring off! Hallo? Hallo?

Angie enters

Angie (*staring at him*) Who are you?

Withers A passing cyclist. Mr Bryce offered me some refreshment ... er ... and the use of the phone. (*He replaces the receiver*)

Angie Where is he?

Withers I think he was looking for you.

Angie Oh. (*Coldly*) Well, when you've finished your drink perhaps you can let yourself out ... (*she turns*)

Withers You're very young.

Angie Am I?

Withers And very attractive.

Angie Thank you.

Withers Don't throw it all away.

Angie I beg your pardon?

Withers You're not happy — I can see that. Would you like to confide in me, as one can in a stranger?

Angie I've no intention of confiding in you, Mr ——?

Withers Withers. Damn. May I ask you a question?

Angie What?

Withers Do you love him?

Angie Who?

Withers Mr Bryce.

Angie What's he been saying?

Withers He loves you. But he needs reassuring. We all need reassuring, for God's sake.

Angie He told you that — a complete stranger?

Withers There's something I must know. Have you ever been unfaithful?

Angie Unfaithful?

Withers With a stoker from H.M.S. Belfast?

Angie Certainly not! What made you say that?

Withers Sorry. I think I'm getting confused. So much has happened today.

Angie You're confused. You're not as confused as I am.

Withers I know you're confused — that's why I'm here. It's not just a bad back, caused by a carelessly erected deckchair, is it? That's your way of making him feel guilty, to hide your own shortcomings. I could give you a good shaking. When are you women going to realize there's no disgrace in frigidity?

Angie Frigidity!

Withers It can be cured. There are books on the subject. You could be a sensual woman again.

Angie Who are you?

Withers (*with a sigh*) I swore I wouldn't tell you but I see I must be absolutely honest. (*He pulls his trousers out of his socks*) I'm not a passing cyclist. I'm a Samaritan.

Angie He rang the Samaritans?

Withers He told me of the dreadful step you were both contemplating, Mrs Bryce.

Angie I see. And he wanted you to talk me out of it.

Withers Precisely. He loves you. He wants you to live.

Angie I fully intend to.

Withers You do? Thank God!

Angie (*grimly*) Although I can't guarantee the continued good health of Mr Bryce.

Withers Have no fear. Once he knows that you love him, that you're going to live, I don't see any problems, Mrs Bryce.

Angie There's just one small snag, Mr Withers.

Withers What's that?

Angie I'm not Mrs Bryce.

Withers What?

Angie So if you'd just finish your orange juice ——

Withers No. I'm not leaving until I've spoken to Mrs Bryce, nor until that carrion of death has left this house.

Vincent, carrying his bag, enters through the french windows

Vincent (*cheerfully*) Someone talking about me? Oh, it's you.

Withers Yes, and I know who you are now, my friend, and what grisly business brings you here.

Vincent I can see you're too clever for me.

Withers Then you can take your pills and potions and ply your despicable trade elsewhere.

Vincent I'm not a tradesman. I'm a professional.

Withers A professional assassin. I don't know how Mrs Bryce could have invited you here.

Vincent That's because you've never had that feeling — that the whole world's having a party and you haven't been invited. That's how she feels and she's got a perfect right to put the cat out, switch off the light and leave a note for the milkman.

Withers No, she hasn't. Life is precious.

Vincent Yours certainly is. House on the river, gold watch, Hush Puppies. You should have a window box in Shepherd's Bush and a wife with a passion for the lower decks.

Withers That's you, but Mrs Bryce has everything to live for.

Vincent Has she? Perhaps she's seen the canker on the rose. (*Glancing at Angie*) Perhaps she's discovered a viper in her bosom. It doesn't really matter. We all live in a house of cards, Mr Withers, and one puff of wind can blow it away. Even yours.

Withers No, I won't listen to your twisted philosophy anymore. I shall stay here until I've seen Mrs Bryce, and when I do, I shall insist that you leave these premises. So you can take your little black bag with its poisonous contents and go.

Vincent (*casually*) Oh, it's not in the bag anymore — it's in the orange juice.

Angie What!

Withers What!

Vincent We were just going to make a start and the orange juice takes the bitterness out of it ... Is something wrong?

Angie But Mr Withers has just drunk from the orange juice.

Vincent Oh no! When was this?

Angie Just now.

Vincent Oh, dear. That's a blow. How do you feel?

Withers (*faintly*) I don't know. I don't feel any different ...

Vincent That's because you're not moving around. Keep still. Don't shake it up, for God's sake. Oh, this is very embarrassing.

Angie Is there an antidote?

Vincent No, but I'm working on it. I'm very sorry.

Withers Sorry! My throat's constricted!

Vincent That's because you're talking too much.

Withers (*hoarsely*) How long?

Vincent Why? Have you got far to go? No, don't answer. Try to avoid any undue exertion. Take the shortest route but avoid any bumpy roads. If the traffic's with you, you could just make it ... (*He guides Withers towards the french windows*)

Withers You've poisoned me!

Vincent Wait a minute. Before we cast the first stone just remember — it's not my fault. I didn't ask you here. I'm afraid this comes from interfering in other people's lives — it never pays. Cast your bread upon the waters and it always comes back soggy. Now, don't say any more. Conserve your energy. (*He opens the french windows*) I'd cut across the lawn if I were you — save time. Nice meeting you, Mr Withers ...

Withers gives him a look of mute reproach and exits

Angie You didn't ... you couldn't ...

Vincent No. (*He grins and pats the bag*) No, it's in the bag, but we didn't want him hanging about spoiling things, did we, miss?

Angie He thought I was Mrs Bryce.

Vincent Funny how we keep making that mistake. Did he want to give you a good shaking?

Angie Yes.

Vincent Yes, I thought he'd want to give you a good shaking. I'd better see him off the premises.

Vincent exits. Walter enters

Walter She's just ... Oh.

Angie You rang for the Samaritans. You never intended to go through with it. It was all talk so that I'd keep seeing you.

Walter It wasn't all talk. I did go through with it — but I couldn't face it twice.

Angie You don't love me — you love her.

Walter I don't. You're the only one I love, Angie. I swear. I would have done it. I ——

Angie Wait a minute. (*She considers*) This gets better and better.

Walter Does it?

Angie Yes.

Walter (*with a sigh*) I thought it might.

Angie That was inspired — phoning the Samaritans, begging them for help. The concerned husband almost out of his mind. Who could accuse you of assisting in her death? You were trying to prevent it. The coroner will probably express his sympathy.

Walter I never thought of that.

Angie Walter — you're a genius. (*She kisses him*)

Celia enters carrying a sealed envelope

Angie sees her before Walter. She moves from his embrace and crosses to Celia. She embraces her with equal warmth. Celia looks surprised

Celia. You too. Both spared. Thank God.

Celia Angie, my dear. I've always found your concern so touching and I'm glad you've come back. I wanted to see you before — Oh, you have little pieces of grass on you ——

Angie Yes, I've been down to Cooper's Bottom.

Celia Cooper's Bottom?

Angie Yes. Thinking ... trying to decide what to do.

Celia Yes. (*She turns to Walter and gives him the envelope*) Put that in a safe place, Walter. It's my new suicide note.

Walter Another one?

Angie Don't do it, Celia.

Celia Please, don't try and dissuade me, Angie. It's too late. Now you're both here — there's something I want to tell you. I've been selfish ——

Walter and Angie protest

— yes, I've been terribly selfish. I've taken too much for granted. I realize now this is one journey I must make alone. Would you be terribly upset, Walter, if I asked you to live?

Walter (*cautiously*) Er, terribly upset? Well, I ...

Angie Don't do it, Celia.

Walter Please, Angie. Let Celia finish.

Celia It's simply that I feel you're only going through with this because you love me, and that would be wrong.

Walter I can see there's no hiding things from you, Celia. Perhaps it would be wrong. I hadn't thought of it like that.

Celia The point is, Walter, do you mind?

Walter No, I don't mind — well, of course I mind — I mind dreadfully. What's life going to be without you? Miserable ... dreary ... unhappy, but if you've really made up your mind, there's nothing more I can say.

Pause

Celia Well, I'll listen to anything you have to say, Walter.

Walter No, it's your life, Celia. And who's to say you're not right? Why wait for the four horsemen of the Apocalypse to come thundering down upon us — and we all know they're just around the corner. War ... pestilence ... famine ... and .... what's the other one?

Celia (*coldly*) Death.

Walter Right. Death. I almost envy you.

Celia Yes. I must say, you make the prospect seem quite attractive. But what will you do without me, Walter? How will you spend the rest of your life?

Walter Life? What life? It won't be a life — just an existence.

Celia And what about you, Angie?

Angie What?

Celia You haven't said "don't do it" for some time.

Angie I can see there's no point in arguing with you, Celia.

Celia I don't mind an argument, Angie.

Angie No, you have that look in your eyes ... a faraway look ... a spiritual, almost ethereal quality ... as if you're already out of reach.

Celia Well, I'm not quite out of reach — not yet. And if you beg me not to do it, even now, Walter ——

Walter No, that wouldn't be fair.

Celia It wouldn't?

Walter No, I have to stop thinking of myself for a change. Of course, I shall miss you dreadfully.

Celia Don't mourn for me, Walter. I don't want that. I don't want you to be unhappy. Why don't you buy a new car — take a holiday?

Walter (*starting*) What?

Celia Go abroad. Spain ... Greece ... West Indies.

Walter (*anxiously*) West Indies?

Celia Don't let him mope, Angie. Make him forget me ——

Walter We could never forget you, could we, Angie?

Angie No.

Walter We'll remember you as you were — a wonderful person.

Angie A very rare person.

Walter Someone who's enriched our lives.

Celia Hardly enriched. I'm leaving most of my money to charity.

Walter What?

Angie That just shows what a wonderful person you are, Celia.

Celia What nice things you're saying about me. It's almost as if I'm dead already.

Angie It shouldn't take long. I suppose the bottle's in the bag.

Walter Do you mean the whole estate, Celia?

Angie I wonder if it's locked? (*She opens the bag*) No, it's not locked — that's careless of him.

Celia and Angie regard each other. Slowly Celia puts her hand in the bag and takes out the bottle

Celia One drink from this and I'll be gone.

Angie That's right, Celia. One drink from that and it'll all be over ...

Celia (*slowly*) I'm going to drink from this bottle and then I'm going to die.

Angie Nothing more certain.

Walter Er, what about the house, Celia?

Celia I'm going to kill myself. Is that all right with you?

Angie Perfectly. We won't stand in your way.

Celia I can see no-one's going to stand in my way.

Vincent enters

Vincent Don't do it, Mrs Bryce.

Angie sighs angrily

I'd like to point out this isn't a game anymore. You're holding a deadly poison. This isn't play-acting.

Celia I've never play-acted, Vincent. I may have rehearsed for this moment most of my life, but it was never play-acting.

Vincent Please. Think again, Mrs Bryce.

Celia (*lightly*) But, Vincent — how can I keep you waiting any longer? You must get to Slough.

Vincent Sod Slough. Don't you see? You're doing it for the wrong reasons — I ——

Vincent breaks off as Celia raises the bottle

Walter Celia!

Angie stamps on his foot

Celia Yes, Walter?

Walter Nothing.

Celia Nothing? Then goodbye, darling. (*She smiles*) I'm glad of one thing — that we made love last night ...

Angie What?

Celia drinks. She stares in surprise, staggers across the room and falls between the desk and sofa. She is partly obscured

She drank it!

Walter She's done it, ~~at last.~~ Is she ...? Is she ...?

Vincent bends over Celia

Vincent Dead? Don't be frightened to use the word, Mr Bryce. Yes — she's dead. She was dead before she hit the ground.

Walter You said there'd be time to walk around and chat.

Vincent I didn't know she was going to drink from the bottle, did I? We usually dilute it. She's had enough to kill a regiment. I was wrong about her. I never thought she'd do it.

Angie Neither did I.

Walter Is that it, then?

Vincent Is what it? You sound disappointed.

Walter It's just that I don't feel any different.

Vincent You weren't meant to. It's Mrs Bryce who's feeling different — if she's feeling anything at all.

Walter (*feeling his pulse*) I'm calmer than I thought I'd be.

Vincent Not as calm as she is.

Angie (*peering over the desk*) She's smiling!

Vincent What did I tell you? Absolute satisfaction.

Walter (*staring at the body*) You're right — she is smiling.

Vincent Yes, almost as if she's having the last laugh on all of us ... as if she already knows something we don't.

Walter Do you mind if we cover her up? It's her eyes ... I ...

Vincent (*with a sigh*) I knew you'd want to cover her up. What is this taboo about death? When I was young we had them in the front parlour for days. Everyone on the street came to see them. Then those who couldn't get in looked through the window.

Angie I'll get something to cover her with.

Angie exits

Vincent (*removing his fingerprints from the furniture*) Well, that concludes our little transaction, Mr Bryce. Remember to leave the suicide note in a prominent position.

Walter Yes. The suicide note — now where did I put it? (*He steps over Celia a couple of times in his search*) Ah yes, Here it is. (*He arranges it on the desk*)

Vincent And a word of warning.

Walter A word of warning? (*He steps over Celia again to cross to Vincent*)

Vincent Do nothing with indecent haste. You know, holidays ... marriage ... babies. Take care, and try and squeeze a few tears out at the inquest.

Walter (*indignantly*) I won't have to squeeze a few tears — she was my wife.

Vincent Yes. Of course.

Angie returns with a cloth

Angie I found a tablecloth. It's only plastic, I'm afraid.

Vincent She's not going to mind. Tuck her in. (*He takes the cloth and covers the body*) Well, goodbye, Mr Bryce. And if I've given satisfaction I hope you'll recommend me to your friends.

Walter You're not leaving?

Vincent Well, there's nothing left for me to do here — unless you want to join her. No, she's dead and gone to glory. Gone but not forgotten:

mourned by a dear friend and a grieving husband. A rose has grown over the wall and blossoms on the other side. The sun has gone from our lives. Take what comfort you can from these words — no extra charge. Oh, that reminds me ... the cheque.

Walter The cheque?

Vincent I destroyed it.

Walter (*relieved*) Thank you.

Vincent Make out another one, would you?

Walter Oh. Yes. (*He crosses to the desk, stepping over Celia again*) Let me see, it was for ——

Vincent Ten thousand.

Walter You said five.

Vincent I said it was flexible.

Walter makes out the cheque

Don't fill the stub in. And don't worry — I won't cash it until after the inquest. Now you've got a lot to do. Phone calls to make. Doctor ... police ... solicitors. It's a busy time for the bereaved. I won't get in your way.

Walter and Angie cross and recross over Celia

Walter Doctor? I don't think I've got his number ...

Angie I've got it.

Walter And my solicitor. What's his home address?

Angie It's in the diary ...

Walter (*frowning*) Do we have to leave her here?

Vincent (*slipping on his coat*) What?

Walter She doesn't look very comfortable. And quite frankly, she's in the way.

Vincent Well, what do you suggest?

Walter What about the bedroom?

Vincent With those stairs and my hernia? She's a dead weight, Mr Bryce. No pun intended. They won't thank you for putting her in the bedroom. Getting a coffin down those stairs would be the devil's own job. No, this is ideal. Straight out the french windows. No problem.

Walter But we've got a great deal to do here ... That's an idea — Take her out through the french windows and put her on the sun-lounger.

Vincent (*grimacing*) The sun-lounger? Is that dignified, Mr Bryce?
Walter We can cover her with the cloth.
Vincent Suppose it rains?
Walter It's plastic.
Vincent (*with a sigh*) All right. Give me a hand.

Vincent and Walter start to pick up the body

Walter Up you come.
Vincent I didn't think she'd be as heavy as this.
Walter She was planning to go on a diet.
Vincent I wish she'd started earlier.

They struggle out through the french windows with the body

Angie shudders

Vincent returns

Angie What's he doing?
Vincent Adjusting the canopy. Keep your eye on him. He'll probably start to twitch in a few minutes. They usually do. Well, I must get to Slough — and it looks like rain. Do you think I could borrow an umbrella?
Angie There's one in the hall.
Vincent Thank you. Goodbye, miss. Nice doing business with you ...

Angie and Vincent exit to the hall. Walter enters and nervously closes the french windows. Angie returns

Walter Has he gone?
Angie Yes.
Walter I need a drink.
Angie Not now, Walter.
Walter (*pouring out a drink*) It's all right for you. You were born with two whiskies inside you — I wasn't. It'll calm my nerves.
Angie Kiss me, Walter.
Walter What?
Angie Kiss me.

They kiss

Walter What's the matter, Angie?

Angie I'm afraid.

Walter Wait a minute — you can't be. I'm the one who's supposed to be afraid. I mean, the whole thing was your idea.

Angie But I never thought she'd do it, Walter.

Walter Angie, if you never thought she'd do it, what have we been breaking our necks for?

Angie Don't you understand? If she hadn't done it you'd have finally seen through her.

Walter But she did do it.

Angie Yes. (*Pause*) Did you think she'd do it?

Walter Yes.

Angie And you stood by?

Walter I didn't stand by. You stamped on my foot. And if we're talking about guilt, who rang Exodus in the first place?

Angie Well, if you'd been prepared to leave her ——

Walter I couldn't leave her.

Angie You couldn't leave the money.

Walter Well, I haven't noticed you turning your nose up at it. What do you think was taking us to Montego Bay? Not that there's going to be much money now. She's probably left it to the dogs' home. I'll have to stop that cheque ——

Angie Walter — you're shouting.

Walter What?

Angie We're quarrelling already. That's what she'd want.

Walter (*taking another drink*) You're right. She's still exercising her power — even now. (*With a shudder*) I can't stay here tonight.

Angie Come to me.

Walter No, it'll arouse suspicion.

Angie Why? "Mr Bryce is under sedation and staying with friends."

Walter No. Vincent said we should do nothing with indecent haste.

Angie (*coldly*) Of course, if you don't want to come ——

Walter Of course I want to come. Are you angry about something?

Angie Why did you make love to her last night?

Walter I didn't.

Angie Then what made her say you did?

Walter I don't know. I suppose she was trying to spoil things between us.

Angie But why would she do that? Unless (*she starts*) — unless she knew.

They stare at each other

Walter She knew! She must have known all along. The suicide note! (*He crosses to the desk and tears open the note*) My God! It's not a suicide note. Listen. (*Reading*) "To whom it may concern. For some weeks now I have had this terrible fear that my husband is trying to poison me. This is since I discovered that he is having an affair with his secretary. I have also found out that he is telling people that I'm suicidal although everyone knows I have a great zest for life. I have been violently sick on several occasions and now try to eat as little as possible. Pray God I'm wrong. Only time will tell ..."

Angie Destroy it.

Walter "P.S. If this note has been destroyed you'll find a copy with my solicitor — to be opened in the event of my death." The bitch. No wonder she was happy to go. She's done for us.

Angie Keep calm, Walter.

Walter Keep calm! I'm hanging on by my fingernails and you say keep calm.

Angie We'll deny everything. She was a neurotic woman. No-one will believe her.

Walter Don't depend on it, Angie. I'd better ring the police.

Angie Before you ring the police, I think there's something we should do.

Walter What's that?

Angie Make love.

Walter What was that, Angie?

Angie Make love.

Walter (*staring at her*) Now?

Angie Yes.

Walter Here?

Angie Yes.

Walter Are you sure? Wouldn't that come under the heading of indecent haste?

Angie We should make love. If we haven't got our love left then all this has been for nothing. We must reaffirm our feelings for each other.

Walter Yes, well, I'd like to reaffirm our feelings for each other, Angie, but under the circumstances, do you think it's going to be terribly successful?

Angie Then she is going to spoil it for us — even from the grave.

Walter That's just it. She's not in the grave yet — she's hardly cold.

Angie I think we should do it now — the sooner the better. After all, we don't know what's going to happen when the police arrive.

Walter It's just that the drink's made me a little woozy ...

Angie (*putting her arms around him*) It's not that. She's made you feel guilty all your life. We must exorcise her ghost.

Walter Don't say ghost, Angie. (*He starts*)

Angie What's the matter?

Walter Her photograph — it's staring at me.

Angie (*placing the photograph face down*) Tomorrow we'll get rid of her clothes. Walter ... (*she leads him to the sofa*) What's the matter now, Walter?

Walter (*uneasily*) Not much room on the sofa, Angie.

Angie All right — the floor.

Walter The floor?

They sink down on to the floor

Walter Angie ... isn't this where she fell?

Angie Yes ...

Walter I thought so ...

The sound of rain striking the windows

Oh no.

Angie What?

Walter It's raining.

Angie (*holding him closer*) Never mind. You do love me, don't you?

Walter Yes.

Angie (*gently*) Well, then ...

They kiss passionately

Celia appears at the window wet and bedraggled. She enters

Walter sees her first. He tries to struggle to his feet

Walter Celia!

Celia points a silent, accusing finger at him. Walter falls backwards

Vincent enters from the hall

CURTAIN

SCENE 2

The same. Evening

The rubber plant has lost most of its leaves

Vincent enters still wearing his mac. He is finishing off a sandwich

Celia enters as Vincent picks up his case

Celia Oh, are you leaving?

Vincent Yes, Mrs Bryce. And thank you once more for your hospitality — the sliced ham was delicious.

Celia It was nothing. I'm the one who should thank you, Vincent — after all, you saved my life.

Vincent (*wincing*) Yes. I would appreciate it if you didn't mention that to anyone — I don't want to get a bad name in the business.

Celia Of course, I understand.

Vincent How's Mr Bryce?

Celia He seems to have stopped twitching. I'm just going to get him a hot water bottle.

Vincent What about the young lady?

Celia (*with a thin smile*) No, I think he'll have to make do with a hot water bottle from now on.

Vincent I mean, has she left?

Celia Yes. She'll never enter this house again. I trusted her and she betrayed me with a kiss. How could Walter have done this to me? It's not as if I've ever been unfaithful to him.

Vincent So I understand. And I was thinking, if you want to even the score ... I think I know the answer.

Celia Oh, what's that?

Vincent Have an affair, Mrs Bryce.

Celia An affair? Oh no.

Vincent Just a brief whirl, Mrs Bryce. Think of the sweet revenge ... the poetic justice.

Celia No, I'd rather not.

Vincent (*pressing*) A fleeting moment of infidelity. Pay him back in his own coin.

Celia Vincent, even if I found the idea of infidelity attractive I simply don't move in those circles.

Vincent (*seductively*) I realize that and all I'm saying is ... if the idea appeals, I'm at your disposal.

Celia (*staring at him*) You?

Vincent Yes.

Celia Is that part of the service, Vincent?

Vincent No — this is personal. And after all, you've nothing to lose now, Mrs Bryce. Do you want to die ... wondering?

Celia Wondering?

Vincent (*temptingly*) What infidelity would have been like? What I would have been like?

Celia (*doubtfully*) No ... I think I'd prefer to wonder, Vincent. Besides, you're wrong: I do have something to lose. I have something to live for. I have to protect Walter from that woman. He needs me.

Vincent He doesn't need you, Mrs Bryce. Do you know how much you're worth to him dead?

Celia Yes, I know ——

Vincent Ten thousand. The price is rising. (*He hands her the cheque*) Note the writing's firm ... the hand legible ... is that the hand of a man who'd be lost without you?

Pause

Celia Do you mind if I keep this, Vincent?

Vincent No. I don't want it. He thought he could buy me. He thought because of my humble origins I had a price. He was wrong.

Celia I'll make a cheque out for something more reasonable ... (*She crosses to the desk and proceeds to make out a cheque*)

Vincent (*disappointed*) But, Mrs Bryce ——

Walter enters. He is dressed for departure

Celia Walter. Where are you going?

Walter I'm leaving.
Celia Don't be ridiculous.
Vincent I'll wait ~~outside~~, Mrs Bryce. *in the kitchen*

Vincent exits

Celia I think you should go and rest, Walter. You look terrible.
Walter I'm leaving, Celia.
Celia Because of that girl?
Walter I happen to love her.
Celia And I loved you, Walter. Until death — and beyond. Twice!
Walter I know, and I'm sorry.
Celia You're sorry! I've often wondered what it would be like to be dead and be able to look down and see what people thought of me. Well, I've had that experience and it wasn't very pleasant. I was shunted out on to the terrace and covered with a plastic table cloth and left in the pouring rain. And when I finally made my return I found my photograph face downwards and you attempting congress on the very spot where I fell.
Walter I don't think it was the exact spot ...
Celia It was like dancing on my grave, Walter. It was certainly out of sight, out of mind where you were concerned. How could I have been so blind! When did all this happen?
Walter When you were at your spiritualist meetings.
Celia My God! I was concerned with the dead when I should have been watching the living.
Walter Well, it's too late now. Vincent was right. The bolts are on the inside. There's nothing to keep me here.
Celia And how do you intend to live?
Walter I'll go back to teaching.
Celia Teaching! They won't have you. They don't give jobs to poisoners.
Walter I'm not a poisoner.
Celia Not yet. But when they read my note with the solicitor ——
Walter You wouldn't.
Celia Try me, Walter. And if that doesn't clinch it, what about the cheque?
Walter Cheque?
Celia You've certainly been busy with the jolly old cheque book, haven't you, Walter? Ten thousand seems to be the going rate at the moment.
Walter (*uneasily*) It wouldn't work.
Celia Well, if you can see any flaws, perhaps you'd point them out.

Walter considers, and then begins to relax

Walter (*smiling*) Yes, I can see a flaw — a big one.
Celia What's that?
Walter You'd have to kill yourself first.
Celia And I will.
Walter Huh!
Celia What was that, Walter?
Walter What?
Celia Did you snort?
Walter (*chuckling*) No.
Celia (*calling*) Vincent.

Vincent enters abruptly, having obviously been listening

Vincent, I want you to give me the poison at once.
Vincent (*with a sigh*) Not again, Mrs Bryce. This is getting monotonous.
Walter Don't worry, Vincent. Things are going to liven up now — for everyone except Celia, that is.
Vincent But I thought we'd settled all this.
Celia Everything's changed. Walter's leaving me.
Vincent I wish you'd make up your mind, Mrs Bryce. First you can't live with him and now you can't live without him.
Celia The bottle, Vincent.
Walter (*helpfully*) Should I get the bag?
Vincent (*coldly*) No. I've been keeping it on my person -- as a precaution.
Celia (*hesitating*) I suppose I'll need something to take it with ...
Walter (*lightly*) What about a dry sherry, Celia? The Amontillado's very good. I'll join you. (*He pours two drinks and hands one to Celia*)
Celia Thank you, Walter. Well, Vincent?
Vincent Are you sure? You don't have to do it now.
Walter Of course not. If Vincent stays much longer he'll talk you to death.

Vincent glares at Walter and adds the poison to Celia's drink

Vincent Do you really think he's worth dying for, Mrs Bryce?
Walter She's not going to die, Vincent. You're wasting your time — she's a born survivor.

Celia Walter ——
Walter I won't be blackmailed, Celia.

The sound of a car horn

That's Angie. She's waiting — I must go.
Celia No — wait.
Walter I can't.
Celia (*hesitating*) You're right, Walter.
Walter What?
Celia I was wrong to threaten you. Tear up the cheque — and the note. I lied. There isn't another copy.
Walter Do you mean that?
Celia Yes.
Walter And you won't do anything silly.

He tries to take her glass but she prevents him

Celia (*smiling bravely*) No, nothing silly. What I'm going to do now is very sensible. I'm going to remove the one obstacle to your happiness. I'm going to give you your freedom, Walter.
Walter But, Celia ——
Celia No. For once I'm calm and rational. I know it's the right thing to do. I've made my decision. I feel at peace.
Vincent Then I won't stay, Mrs Bryce. Normally I enjoy my work but I'm not proud of my part in this. I seem to have lost my zest for it, somehow. I'll come back ... later. Goodbye.
Celia Goodbye. Oh, Vincent. Would you ask Angie to come in for a moment?
Vincent Certainly.

Vincent exits

Walter Why do you want to see Angie?
Celia Why not, Walter? Let's have one last drink together as friends.
Walter What are you going to say to her?
Celia Don't worry. I'm not angry anymore. It's too late for that. Pour her a drink, Walter.

Walter pours out a drink

Walter Are you sure you're not angry?

Celia Of course not. I'm not bitter anymore. She's won and I've lost. I just want her to know that. I don't reproach her for what's happened. She couldn't help her emotions, Walter. Is she coming?

Walter crosses to the window and looks out. Celia deftly changes her glass with Angie's and returns to her seat

Walter (*turning*) Yes — she's coming.

Celia Oh, good.

Angie enters

Angie (*coldly*) Well, what is it?

Celia Don't look so stern, Angie. I thought we could have one last drink together. (*Significantly*) One for the road, Angie.

Angie You mean ...?

Celia Yes. You're looking at a lonely, defeated woman. There's nothing left for me now. Walter, pass Angie her glass. Careful. Don't spill it. Now, what should we drink to?

Walter You don't have to go through with it, Celia.

Angie Don't stop her, Walter — if you can't face up to this moment you'll never be free of her.

Walter Angie, I've faced up to this moment twice, and she's still here. My nerves can't take much more.

Angie Don't weaken now.

Celia She's right. Listen to her, Walter. So young, so strong — so diamond hard. She'll be good for you. I was always too weak. Now, what shall we drink to? I know, the second Mrs Bryce. Bottoms up, Angie.

They raise their glasses. Angie hesitates and lowers her glass

Angie No.

Celia (*disappointed*) No?

Angie No, don't drink to me, Celia — it would be too hypocritical.

Celia Oh. Then let's drink to death. To death, everyone.

They raise their glasses. Walter lowers his

Walter No.

Celia No?

Walter Not to death.

Celia Then let's drink to life. Your life together — you and Angie. Who
knows what the future holds? Your life may be long and happy ... it may
be tragically short, but whatever happens I hope you'll never regret the
way you wounded me with your cruel deception.

Angie goes to put her glass down

Don't put your glass down, Angie — you'll mark the surface. To your
future.

Walter No.

Angie She won't do it, Walter.

Celia (*angrily*) Will someone give me the chance for God's sake? Are we
going to drink or not?

Angie Yes, I'll give you a toast, Celia. To love.

Celia To love. Bye, Angie.

Walter No! Don't do it. I'll stay.

Celia What?

Angie Walter!

Celia Walter, are you sure?

Angie You fool. Don't you see? She wouldn't have done it.

Walter I'm sorry. I couldn't take the chance.

Celia (*soothingly*) Now let's put our glasses down and talk about this ...

Walter I couldn't stand by and see her destroy herself. I've hurt her
enough.

Angie You don't want to hurt her, but you don't care how you hurt me.

Celia Now, let me take your glass, Angie — before you spill it ——

Angie All those promises — all those lies. I bet you've been humping her
all along.

Celia (*staring at her*) Humping? What does she mean, Walter?

Walter I just couldn't face another suicide attempt. It's been a long day.

Celia Angie — your glass. (*She finally retrieves Angie's glass*)

Angie (*scornfully*) You don't know what love is — either of you. Well,
I'll show you. If she won't drink it, I will. (*She snatches up Celia's glass
and drinks*)

They stare at her in surprise

Walter Angie!

Angie (*shocked*) I wish I hadn't done that.

Walter Angie, my poor darling — keep still — put your fingers down your throat. I'll ring for a doctor — an ambulance. I'll dial nine-nine-nine.

Celia Don't fuss, Walter.

Walter Don't fuss! Angie's just poisoned herself.

Celia No, she hasn't.

Walter What do you mean?

Celia (*hesitating*) Well, she doesn't look poisoned to me.

Walter How do you feel, Angie?

Angie I don't feel poisoned.

Walter But I saw him put it in the glass ...

Celia Perhaps she's just slightly poisoned ...

Angie No, I feel fine.

Celia Wonderful. What resistance. It would have probably killed an older woman.

Walter But I saw him put it in the glass. I didn't take my eyes off it. Well, except when ~~I turned to the window~~ —— *into the hall*

Angie and Walter stare at each other and then at Celia

Celia What are you staring at?

Walter If it isn't in that glass then where is it ...?

Angie Celia, since I've taken your drink, perhaps you'd care to take mine?

Celia (*abruptly*) No.

Angie You tried to kill me.

Walter You switched the glasses.

Celia She's no good for you, Walter. I was trying to protect you. She's too young.

Angie Yes, and if it had been left to you I wouldn't have got any older. (*Confidently*) Are you coming, Walter?

Walter Yes. Goodbye, Celia.

Celia (*desperately*) Walter, if you go I will take this drink — I swear. See — I'm taking it. Say something, Walter.

Walter smiles slowly

Walter Cheers, Celia.

Angie and Walter exit

Celia holds the glass to her lips for a long moment and then puts it down gently on the coffee table. She crosses to the desk, sits and slumps forward wearily

Vincent enters. He sees Celia slumped forward and notes Angie's empty glass on the desk. He sighs and wipes the glass clean of fingerprints. He crosses and pours himself a sherry. He selects several books from the bookcase and drops them into his bag

He becomes aware of Celia staring at him

Vincent Good heavens, Mrs Bryce. You gave me quite a turn. You certainly keep bouncing back, don't you? What resilience.

Celia Don't mock me, Vincent.

Vincent I'm not mocking you. I'm astonished. Mr Bryce was right — you are indestructible.

Celia (*irritably*) I didn't take it.

Vincent I gathered that.

Celia But I shall.

Vincent Of course.

Celia Probably tomorrow.

Vincent Why not? I hear the weather's going to be abysmal tomorrow.

Celia I just didn't feel like it. You don't always feel like it.

Vincent You're not ready yet. Anyone can see that.

Celia I will be. After all, there's nothing to keep me here — now Walter's gone. I shall be very lonely.

Vincent No need to be lonely. There's plenty of men I know who'd give their right arm to shack up here.

Celia I beg your pardon?

Vincent Look out there, Mrs Bryce. See the daffodils and the other ones, not quite as yellow?

Celia Narcissi.

Vincent Aren't they a picture? And the primroses and the violets ... and those bluebell things ...

Celia Hyacinths.

Vincent And the yellow bushes of ——

Celia Forsythia.

Vincent (*sharply*) I know it's forsythia, Mrs Bryce. What I'm saying is that you've got a lovely spot here.

Celia You should see it in high summer.

Vincent I'd love to.

Celia The walls are draped with wisteria and clematis. The whole house is filled with the scent of flowers.

Vincent (*enviously*) The scent of flowers ... all I get is fried rice — even on Sundays. I can just imagine Sundays here, Mrs Bryce. Roast beef cooking in the kitchen and the sound of church bells from the village ... none of that interminable, oriental chatter. A day when the kitchen smells of the garden and the garden smells of roast beef and gravy. A man could be very comfortable here on a Sunday morning. He could take a slim volume from the bookshelf and sit with an ice-cold drink out there on the terrace ... and listen to the birdsong. Is there birdsong, Mrs Bryce?

Celia Oh, yes. And soon there'll be the sound of the cuckoo across the meadow. Not that I shall be here to listen to it.

Vincent (*suddenly*) Why not, Mrs Bryce?

Celia What?

Vincent I've an idea. Why not wait for the first cuckoo and then do it?

Celia Do what?

Vincent Kill yourself. That should give you enough time to think about it. Make proper preparations.

Celia What a good idea. That's what I'll do. I'll wait for the sound of the first cuckoo and then I'll kill myself. I'm glad that's settled. I feel better already.

Vincent Good. Now I'm afraid I must take my leave ——

Celia You're not going?

Vincent I must get to Slough.

Celia Oh, I'd forgotten. That means I'll be here alone.

Vincent Not necessarily. Why not come with me?

Celia You mean to Slough?

Vincent Why not?

Celia Won't I be in the way?

Vincent No — you'll be an asset. Although I should warn you he may be in a state. He could be prostrate with despair.

Celia Yes, I suppose the scene could be harrowing.

Vincent Harrowing's hardly the word, Mrs Bryce.

Celia I'll get my coat. (*Pause*) Suppose he's changed his mind?
Vincent Well, I'm sure we could soon change it back again. (*He raises his glass*) Here's to Slough, Mrs Bryce.
Celia To Slough.
Vincent And after ... (*He drinks*)

Celia exits

The telephone rings. Vincent answers

Vincent Hallo?...What?... (*He frowns*) Samaritans? Sod off. (*He slams the phone down. He takes another drink*)

Celia returns with her coat

Celia Ready, Vincent?
Vincent Yes. (*He rises and stops*) Funny — my leg seems to have gone to sleep. I suppose it's sitting around all day.
Celia You must be tired. I'll bring the car round to the front. It'll be a lovely evening for a drive. Look at the sky. I think you're wrong about tomorrow. Red sky at night, shepherd's delight, Vincent.
Vincent (*looking thoughtfully at his feet*) Mrs Bryce, when you said you didn't take the drink, where did you put it? I suppose it was the rubber plant again?
Celia (*tidying the room*) No. I put it down somewhere.
Vincent (*worried*) But the empty glass.
Celia No, that was Angie's.
Vincent Oh. Do you remember exactly where you put it?
Celia (*absently*) I'm not sure ... over there somewhere. Will I do like this? I was going to wear black, but I thought why be gloomy?
Vincent (*concerned*) You said you put it over there. (*Brightly*) Dare I hope it's the one on the drinks tray?
Celia What? No, that was Walter's.
Vincent That's Walter's. And that one was Angie's. Now I put my glass on the coffee table ...
Celia Oh, I remember — I put it on the coffee table.
Vincent (*starting*) Coffee table!
Celia Is something the matter?
Vincent Only that I feel rather tired ... almost leaden ... I ... (*He crosses the room with difficulty*)

Celia Well, it's been a long day. (*She locks the french windows*) I'll drive. You rest in the back. You know, I feel quite excited. I feel a sense of optimism ...

Vincent sinks slowly to the floor

I'm filled with a new vitality. (*She turns*) Vincent, is something wrong? Why are you lying on the carpet? Are you so fatigued?
Vincent (*struggling to speak*) Mrs Bryce ...
Celia Vincent — your voice. (*She crouches over him and touches his hands*) Your hands — they're cold.
Vincent (*straightening up*) My God!
Celia What is it?
Vincent I can smell fried rice! (*He falls back dead*)
Celia (*staring down at him uneasily*) Er, Vincent ... Vincent?

Across the garden comes the distant sound of a cuckoo. The Lights fade

CURTAIN

FURNITURE AND PROPERTY LIST

ACT I
SCENE 1

On stage: Adam fireplace
Bookcases with books
Large rubber plant
Easy chairs
Sofa
Coffee table
Ashtray
Table
Drinks tray. *On it:* sherry, orange juice, glasses, red goblet, lemon slices, shaker
Desk. *On it:* cheque book, cheque, sheaf of letters, telephone, holiday brochure, photograph of Celia
Box of tissues
Bin
Cardigan

Off stage: Black bag containing bottle of poison, packet of crisps (Vincent)

Personal: Vincent: sandwiches in coat pocket; handkerchief
Walter: handkerchief

SCENE 2

Set: Rubber plant with one dead leaf

Strike: Rubber plant

Personal: Vincent: black bag as before, containing cigarettes, cigarette lighter
Withers: wrist-watch

ACT II
SCENE 1

Set: Yellowed rubber plant missing several leaves

Strike: Rubber plant with one dead leaf

Off stage: Sealed envelope containing a letter (Celia)
Plastic tablecloth (Angie)

Personal: **Vincent:** black bag as before

SCENE 2

Set: Blackening rubber plant with only a few leaves

Strike: Yellowed rubber plant missing several leaves

Off stage: Sandwich (Vincent)
Coat (Celia)

Personal: **Vincent:** black bag as before

LIGHTING PLOT

ACT I, SCENE 1

No cues

ACT I, SCENE 2

No cues

ACT II, SCENE 1

No cues

ACT II, SCENE 2

Cue 1   The distant sound of a cuckoo   (Page 69)
             The lights fade

EFFECTS PLOT

ACT I

No cues

ACT II

Cue 1	**Walter:** "I thought so ..." *Sound of rain striking the windows*	(Page 57)
Cue 2	**Walter:** "I won't be blackmailed, Celia." *Car horn*	(Page 62)
Cue 3	**Celia** exits *The telephone rings*	(Page 68)
Cue 4	**Celia:** "Er, Vincent ... Vincent?" *The distant sound of a cuckoo*	(Page 69)

Lightning Source UK Ltd.
Milton Keynes UK
UKOW06f0051250117
292821UK00001B/121/P

9 780573 018411